The BEAUTIFUL, The SUBLIME, and The PICTURESQUE

British Influences on American Landscape Painting

February 18 to April 8, 1984

Washington University Gallery of Art

St. Louis, Missouri

Co-Curators

Joseph D. Ketner II   Michael J. Tammenga

This exhibition, publication, and related programs
have been made possible by:

The Institute of Museum Services

The Arts and Education Council of Greater St. Louis

The Steinberg Charitable Trust

The Hortense Lewin Art Fund

Cover:
Frederic E. Church.
Sierra Nevada de Santa Marta,
1883 (no. 62)

Library of Congress Catalog Card Number 83-51827
ISBN 0-936316-05-5
Designed by Hawthorne/Wolfe Design Consultants
Type set by The First Impression, Inc.
Printed by Keeler Morris
Bound by J. Lewin Bookbinding Co.

Table of Contents

THE BUTLER INSTITUTE OF AMERICAN ART, *Youngstown, Ohio*

FORT WAYNE MUSEUM OF ART, *Ft. Wayne, Indiana*

INDIANAPOLIS MUSEUM OF ART, *Indianapolis, Indiana*

MEMPHIS BROOKS MUSEUM OF ART, *Memphis, Tennessee*

MISSOURI HISTORICAL SOCIETY, *St. Louis, Missouri*

MUSEUM OF FINE ARTS, *Boston, Massachusetts*

MUSKEGON MUSEUM OF ART, *Muskegon, Michigan*

THE NELSON-ATKINS MUSEUM OF ART, *Kansas City, Missouri*

THE NEW-YORK HISTORICAL SOCIETY, *New York, New York*

THE SAINT LOUIS ART MUSEUM, *St. Louis, Missouri*

THE SHELDON SWOPE ART GALLERY, *Terre Haute, Indiana*

THE J.B. SPEED ART MUSEUM, *Louisville, Kentucky*

SPENCER MUSEUM OF ART, THE UNIVERSITY OF KANSAS, *Lawrence, Kansas*

MR. AND MRS. J. GRAY SWEENEY, *Grand Rapids, Michigan*

THE TAFT MUSEUM, *Cincinnati, Ohio*

UNIVERSITY OF IOWA, SPECIAL COLLECTIONS, *Iowa City, Iowa*

THE UNIVERSITY OF MISSOURI, MUSEUM OF ART AND ARCHAEOLOGY, *Columbia, Missouri*

VOSE GALLERIES, *Boston, Massachusetts*

WASHINGTON UNIVERSITY, ART AND ARCHITECTURE LIBRARY, *St. Louis, Missouri*

WASHINGTON UNIVERSITY, THE JOHN M. OLIN LIBRARY, *St. Louis, Missouri*

YALE CENTER FOR BRITISH ART, *New Haven, Connecticut*

*T*HE *B*EAUTIFUL, *The Sublime, and The Picturesque: British Influences on American Landscape Painting* is inspired by some of Washington University's greatest treasures, its American landscape paintings. Several of these paintings have been in St. Louis since the opening of the St. Louis School and Museum of Fine Arts, a Department of Washington University, in May 1881. Two landscapes were especially prominent at that time, one thought to be Joseph M.W. Turner and one by Frederic E. Church, the giants of their profession. Contemporary opinion of their accomplishments epitomized the divergence of European and American aesthetic preferences. The British Turner (1775-1851) was generally characterized as the father of modern landscape painting, while the American Church (1826-1900) was venerated by his contemporaries as a living master.

In his review of the 1881 exhibition inaugurating the St. Louis School and Museum of Fine Arts, the local art critic William M. Bryant differentiated four subject areas among the 143 paintings: history, genre, animal, and landscape. These categories echoed the traditional European academic hierarchy, which ranked history painting most consequential. Furthermore, about three-quarters of the works in the exhibition had been painted by Europeans. In fact, it was the lack of work by his countrymen available in St. Louis that had stimulated Wayman Crow to establish the St. Louis School and Museum of Fine Arts with the ambition that the school "foster a distinctively American type of art."

Bryant concluded his review by turning to landscape painting and stating: "In the final outcome it is *spiritual* light, and that alone, that illuminates the world—that alone by which there is any seeing." He then proceeded to compare the Venetian canal scene attributed to Turner and Church's *Mount Desert Island, Maine*, 1865 (cat. no. 59). Church's dramatic panorama of dawn breaking over the Maine coast was one of the prized possessions of Charles Parsons, a St. Louis merchant. Parsons was soon to purchase an even more monumental canvas from Church, *Sierra Nevada de Santa Marta*, 1883 (no. 62), and eventually bequeathed both paintings, plus a hundred more European and American works, to Washington University. Considering the Venetian scene, Bryant noted the "vagueness of form and the indefiniteness of significance characterizing so much of his [Turner's] work." Church, on the other hand, presents the clear triumph of light over dark, and, therefore, "Church possesses, if not a more powerful, assuredly a clearer, more penetrating spirit; and as a landscape-painter, strictly speaking, he is distinctly and decidedly above and beyond Turner."

American artists had long been compared to their British counterparts. Bryant's review reflects the growing esteem for American landscape painters, who, by his time, had come to be regarded as equal or superior to Turner and the Europeans. Generations of British influence on American art had profoundly affected the development of the Hudson River School. Three British aesthetic conceptions — the Beautiful, the Sublime, and the Picturesque — had been appropriated and transformed by American artists to express the aesthetic and spiritual ideals of their own country. Frederic Church gave form to the American vision of the New World illuminated in "spiritual light" and to the spirit of Manifest Destiny.

The Beautiful, The Sublime, and The Picturesque was conceived by Michael J. Tammenga, the first participant in a curatorial internship program funded by the Institute of Museum Services, a federal agency administering to the unique needs of museums of all types. As Curatorial Assistant, Mr. Tammenga concentrated on nineteenth-century European and American art and proposed this exhibition to provide a context for understanding a group of the University's major landscape paintings. Joseph D. Ketner II, Curator and Registrar, collaborated with Mr. Tammenga in developing the proposal into a loan exhibition drawn primarily from the Midwest. With the enthusiastic support of the lenders, they now present a unique framework in which to appreciate a few of the intriguing relationships that existed between British and American landscape painting during the late eighteenth and nineteenth centuries. We proudly present this exhibition to our community and the Institute of Museum Services as evidence of a fruitful internship program and the Washington

University Gallery of Art's continuing commitment to scholarship and education.

Realization of an exhibition depends ultimately on the generosity of lenders who must part with prized art works for months at a time. We are grateful, therefore, to the lenders for sharing their treasures with our community. Many of the participating institutions also welcomed us into their storerooms and shared knowledge about their holdings. James Bell, Director of The New-York Historical Society, Ruth Meyer, Director of The Taft Museum, and Carol Troyen, Assistant Curator of Paintings at the Museum of Fine Arts, Boston, offered much good advice and moral support. Mary Carver, Registrar of The J.B. Speed Art Museum, and Douglas Hyland, Director of the Memphis Brooks Museum of Art, encouraged the project by their thoughtful responses to our inquiries.

Encompassing more than a century of art history, the quantity of resources for this project was almost as massive as the sublime mountains in some of the paintings, and would have presented insurmountable barriers without the guidance offered us on research expeditions. Anthony Janson, Senior Curator, and Martin Krause, Curator of Prints and Drawings, at the Indianapolis Museum of Art, provided a wealth of information and ideas for which we are grateful. Patrick Noon, Curator of Prints and Drawings, and Malcolm Cormack, Curator of Paintings, introduced us to the unique resources of the Yale Center for British Art, and we thank them both for increasing our awareness of the nuances of the subject. In developing the broad bibliography for this exhibition, we were guided by the examples of William H. Gerdts and Louis Hawes, who together expedited our research immeasurably.

We are grateful to our friends in St. Louis for assistance in publishing this catalog. Terry Van Schaik edited the manuscript with exceptional commitment and acumen. We thank Doug Wolfe for an elegant catalog format which serves the intent of the project. Natalie Mondschein, Administrative Secretary, and Rebecca Haidt, Student Curatorial Assistant, have our appreciation for their enthusiasm and dedication while bearing the burden of typing correspondence and catalog drafts. For his meticulous handling of the show we thank David Lobbig, Gallery Facilities Manager.

The Arts and Education Council of Greater St. Louis provided funds for the interpretive brochure distributed in the exhibition gallery. Support for this project was also provided by the Steinberg Charitable Trust.

The generosity of Mr. Tobias Lewin, who established The Hortense Lewin Art Fund in memory of his wife, enabled the realization of this, the inaugural Lewin Exhibition. As the first endowment fund designated for special exhibitions, the Hortense Lewin Art Fund also offers the promise of distinguished special projects in the future. We are privileged and delighted to present this exhibition as testament to the Lewins' dedication to their alma mater and commitment to encouraging enjoyment of the arts in St. Louis.

Gerald D. Bolas
Director
Washington University
Gallery of Art

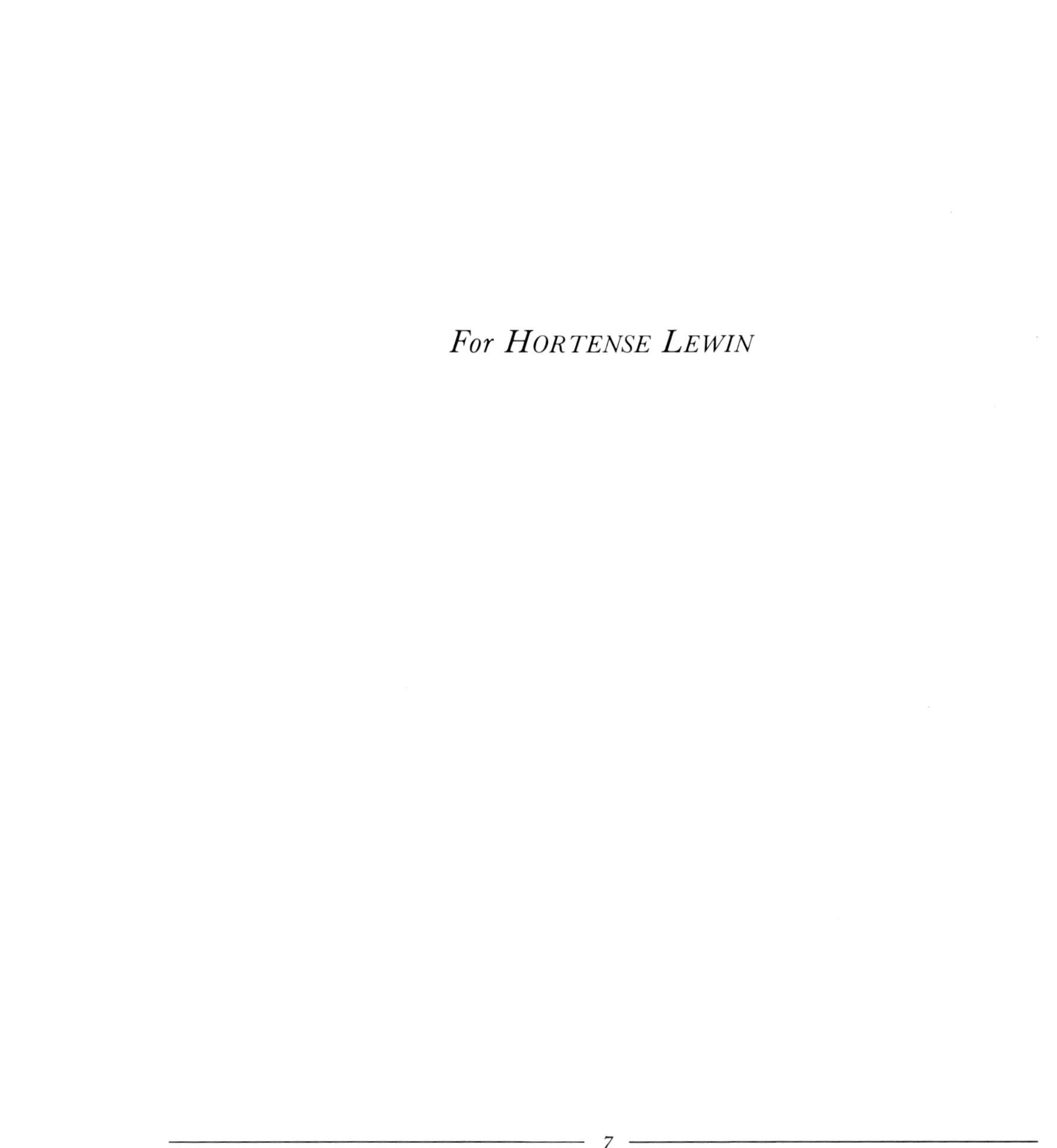

For Hortense Lewin

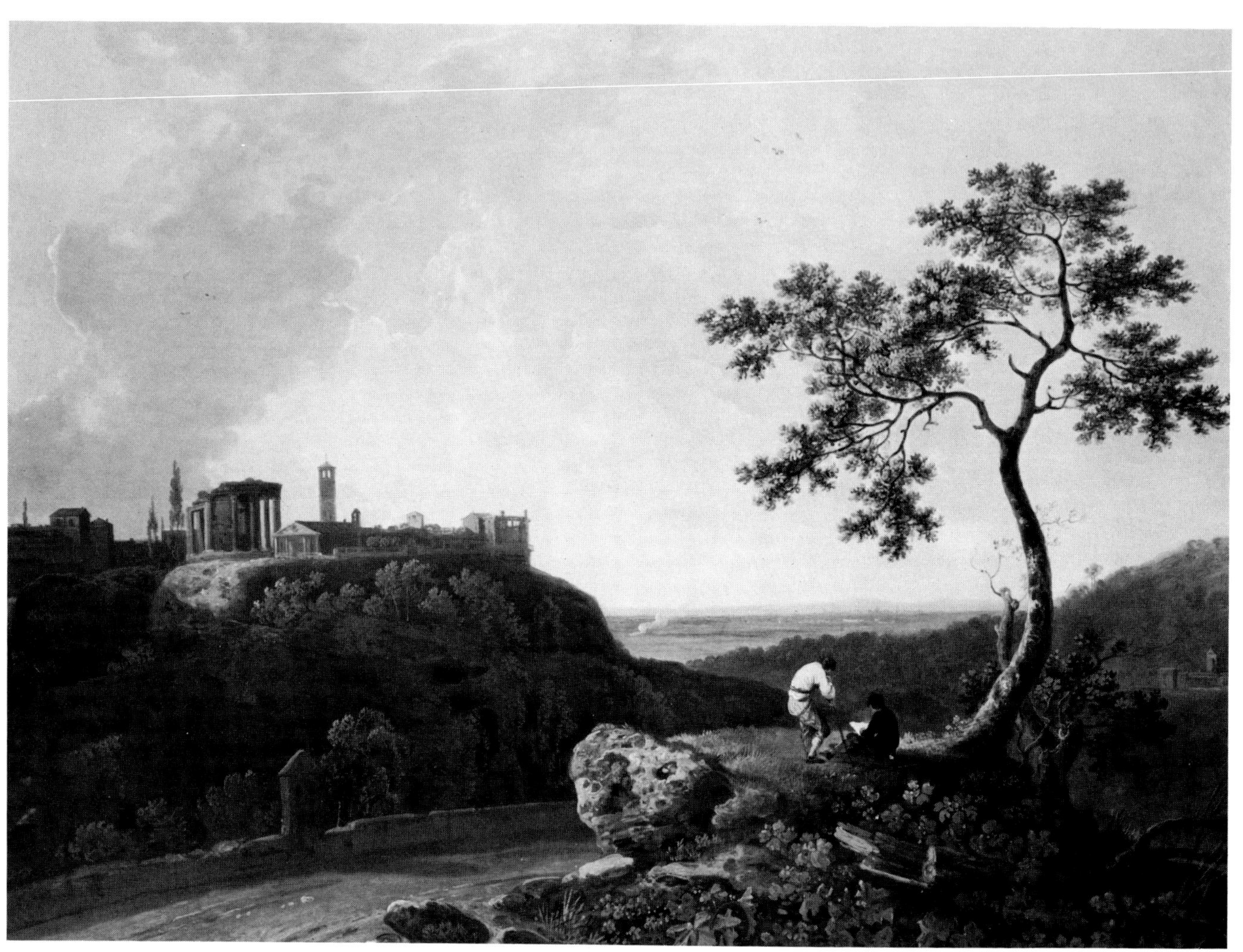

Richard Wilson. *Tivoli: Temple of the Sibyl and the Campagna*, 1763-67 (no.1)

TTEMPTING to stimulate interest in the exploration and appreciation of American landscape, John Hill introduced his *Picturesque Views of American Scenery* (Philadelphia: 1820; catalog nos. 27 & 28) with a challenge to Americans:

In no quarter of the globe are the majesty and loveliness of nature more strikingly conspicuous than in America. The vast regions which are comprised in or subjected to the republic represent to the eye every variety of the beautiful and sublime. Our lovely mountains and almost boundless prairies, our broad and magnificent rivers, the unexampled magnitude of our cataracts, the wild grandeur of our western forests, and the rich and variegated tints of our autumnal landscapes, are unsurpassed by any of the boasted scenery of other countries.[1]

Nevertheless, the natural wonders had been largely ignored by American artists. This situation was far different from Europe where "picturesque views" of scenery, from the Alps to the "tame level of the English landscape," were commonplace. "America only, of all the countries of civilized man, is unsung and undescribed."[2] This state of cultural affairs reversed completely during the next fifty years. Two generations of American landscape painters, popularly known as the Hudson River School, had embraced the subjects offered in Hill's *Picturesque Views* and established a tradition of American landscape painting. By 1865 an English critic could announce that "America has long maintained supremacy in the landscape art; perhaps indeed, its landscape artists surpass those of England; certainly we have no painter who can equal the works of [Frederic E.] Church."[3]

The artist who painted the watercolors for Hill's *Picturesque Views* was an immigrant English artist, Joshua Shaw (ca. 1777-1860). Shaw had arrived in America just three years earlier as a professional landscape painter versed in the contemporary British styles. From 1819-1820, he traveled extensively through New England and along the eastern seaboard, painting a variety of scenes that Hill describes in terms of beautiful, sublime, and picturesque characteristics, pictorial qualities deeply rooted in 18th-century British landscape painting and aesthetics.

Although British art has long been acknowledged as a catalyst for early American arts, the direct influence of the British on the American landscape vision is uncharted territory.[4] This exhibition's title echoes the important book by Walter Hipple, *The Beautiful, The Sublime, and The Picturesque in Eighteenth Century British Aesthetic Theory* (1957), that offers the most comprehensive analysis in print of these theories. The Washington University Gallery of Art's project takes these aesthetic conceptions as points of departure for investigating British influences in American landscape painting. The following essay will briefly survey British landscape painting styles and aesthetics, their transfer to America, and American artists' transformations of the styles and ideas within the Hudson River School.

The theories of the beautiful, the sublime, and the picturesque were predominantly evident in British and American landscape painting from approximately 1750 to the Civil War. Further, many of the leading artists of the second generation of the Hudson River School painted in these aesthetic modes well beyond the third quarter of the nineteenth century. Certain paintings, therefore, are included in this exhibition despite their late dates. Pure landscape, the most characteristic subject matter of the Hudson River School, is isolated here for consideration. No historical landscapes, topographical views, townscapes, or marines appear in this discussion. Granted, these are vital areas of early American landscape art, but they involve histories of their own and different aspects of European influence. The impact of British writer John Ruskin (1819-1900) has also been excluded, since he rejected beautiful, sublime, and picturesque conventions in favor of a "truth to nature." For our purposes, it is important to acknowledge two of Ruskin's key influences on American landscape painters: his belief in the moral value of nature, and his promotion of Joseph M.W. Turner as the pre-eminent contemporary artist.

On the crest of romantic literary enthusiasm for landscape

as a medium of poetic expression, British artists around 1750 elevated landscape painting to the rank of an esteemed genre. Richard Wilson was the first Englishman to establish a career as a landscape painter. He formulated his style on the examples of 17th-century classical masters to create ''beautiful'' landscapes. Basically, the ''beautiful'' and ''classical'' are interchangeable terms to describe a serene, calm landscape consisting of idealized natural forms arranged in a balanced composition. An arcadian, pastoral mood permeates these landscapes, typically bathed in the soothing half-light of a sunrise or sunset. Contemporaneously, the realistic style of the 17th-century Dutch landscapists inspired other English artists to depict their native countryside. Thomas Gainsborough's works were seminal in motivating artists to sketch uncultivated rural nature and to compose from those sketches ''picturesque'' scenes. Picturesque qualities were found in rough, craggy trees and foliage, sharp contrasts of light and shadow, and rustic anecdotes. Writers and artists of the picturesque stimulated an interest in the variety and contrast of visible, rather than idealized, nature. The ''sublime'' was the most distinctive aspect of British romantic landscape art. Tremendous mountains, deep valleys, and cataclysmic storms were the most typical subjects of sublime landscapes. Terror and wonder engendered the emotional bases of a sublime aesthetic response to wild nature. Among the artists of terrific mountain scenes, Joseph M.W. Turner revolutionized the approaches to the sublime in nature.

After the close of the Revolutionary War Americans were concerned with developing a national cultural identity. Faced with the unique character of the American wilderness and lacking an indigenous landscape tradition, Americans turned to their British heritage for stylistic precedents. British styles and ideas were transferred to America along four main routes: immigrant British artists, American artists traveling abroad, the first American art academies, and the distribution of British prints and books. Americans tended to integrate the British modes into a single work, and the original aesthetic distinctions were often blurred. Unlike the British, who usually conveyed one stylistic mode, the Americans freely mixed the beautiful, sublime, and picturesque approaches in their paintings. Turner, considered in his day the premier landscape artist, was the most diverse of the British and painted works in each of the three styles. On the other side of the Atlantic, Thomas Cole was the pivotal Hudson River School artist whose works encompassed the range of stylistic possibilities. His example established the precedent for successive generations of Hudson River School artists working with the beautiful, the sublime, and the picturesque. The correspondences between British and American landscape painting in these modes are striking and offer a unique perspective on the development of American art.

*I*N THE LATE 1760s, Lord Shelburne commissioned three landscape paintings for the decoration of the drawing-room at his Wiltshire home, Bowood. For the task he selected Richard Wilson (1713-82), Thomas Gainsborough (1727-88), and George Barret (1732?-84), whose paintings were "intended to lay the foundation of a school of British landscapes, the want of which has often been lamented."[5] As John Hayes notes, this commission indicates the serious commitment with which a growing number of patrons encouraged native talent in landscape painting.[6] The diversity of the commissioned paintings reflects the three primary stylistic options available to mid-18th-century British landscape painters: classical, topographical, and picturesque. Richard Wilson, the first English artist to specialize in landscape painting, executed an Italianate composition of *Apollo and the Seasons.* (A version is in the Indianapolis Museum or Art.) His painting presents an idealized vision of nature with gods at leisure in a harmoniously balanced composition bathed in warm, golden light. It is a testament to the hold of the classical landscape tradition on the mid-18th-century imagination.

The painting commissioned from Barret, though it remains unidentified, was probably a topographical view like those upon which he had founded his reputation. Topographic "estate portraits" and views of British towns mapped out the salient details of a landscape with a dispassionate attention to accuracy and inclusiveness. This branch of landscape painting was one of the few open to interested early 18th-century British artists and was a firmly established tradition by the time of Lord Shelburne's commission. The third painting, Thomas Gainsborough's *Returning from Market,* ca. 1767-8 (Toledo Museum of Art), concentrates on the poetic qualities of rural English farmers in their natural setting. This painting is a signpost indicating a change in tastes from idealized and topographical landscapes towards a romantic appreciation of the countryside.

*T*HE *BEAUTIFUL*
The most influential landscape painter at the time of Lord Shelburne's commissions was Richard Wilson, the father of English landscape painting. Wilson studied the landscape masters while on his grand tour in the 1750s. Inspired by the example of 17th-and early 18th-century masters in his choice of subject and composition, Wilson's *Tivoli: Temple of the Sibyl and the Campagna,* 1763-67 (no. 1), exemplifies the classical ideal of a beautiful landscape. The serene scene with ruins on a bluff overlooking the Campagna creates a mood of pastoral repose. Framed by the masses of the tree in the foreground and the hills in the middleground, the balanced composition reinforces a sense of natural order. The eye follows a series of diagonals past the various landscape motifs toward the soft light at the horizon. Tivoli was the ancient capitol of the Sabines and became an important center for Roman literature. By the mid-18th-century Tivoli was an integral part of every artist's grand tour. Aware that Tivoli had been praised for its beauty by ancient poets and painted by Gaspard, Poussin, and other classical landscapists, Wilson stresses his identification with artistic tradition by including in the foreground the image of an artist, perhaps himself, recording the scene in emulation of the masters.

As a founding member of the Royal Academy in 1768 and the chief proponent of the "grand style" in landscape painting, Wilson was aware of academic principles governing art. According to academic theory, painting's chief aim was the presentation of ideal beauty. The standard manual on decorum in the visual arts, Charles Alphonse DuFresnoy's *The Art of Painting* (1668, no. 6), expressed the opinion that "Our business is to imitate the Beauties of Nature, as the Ancients have done before us."[7] Most important is the choice of noble subjects, the expression of which should be "comfortable to the Texts of ancient Authors, to Customs, and to Times."[8] An art of the beautiful and noble drew upon the ideal qualities of "nature which is at present before your

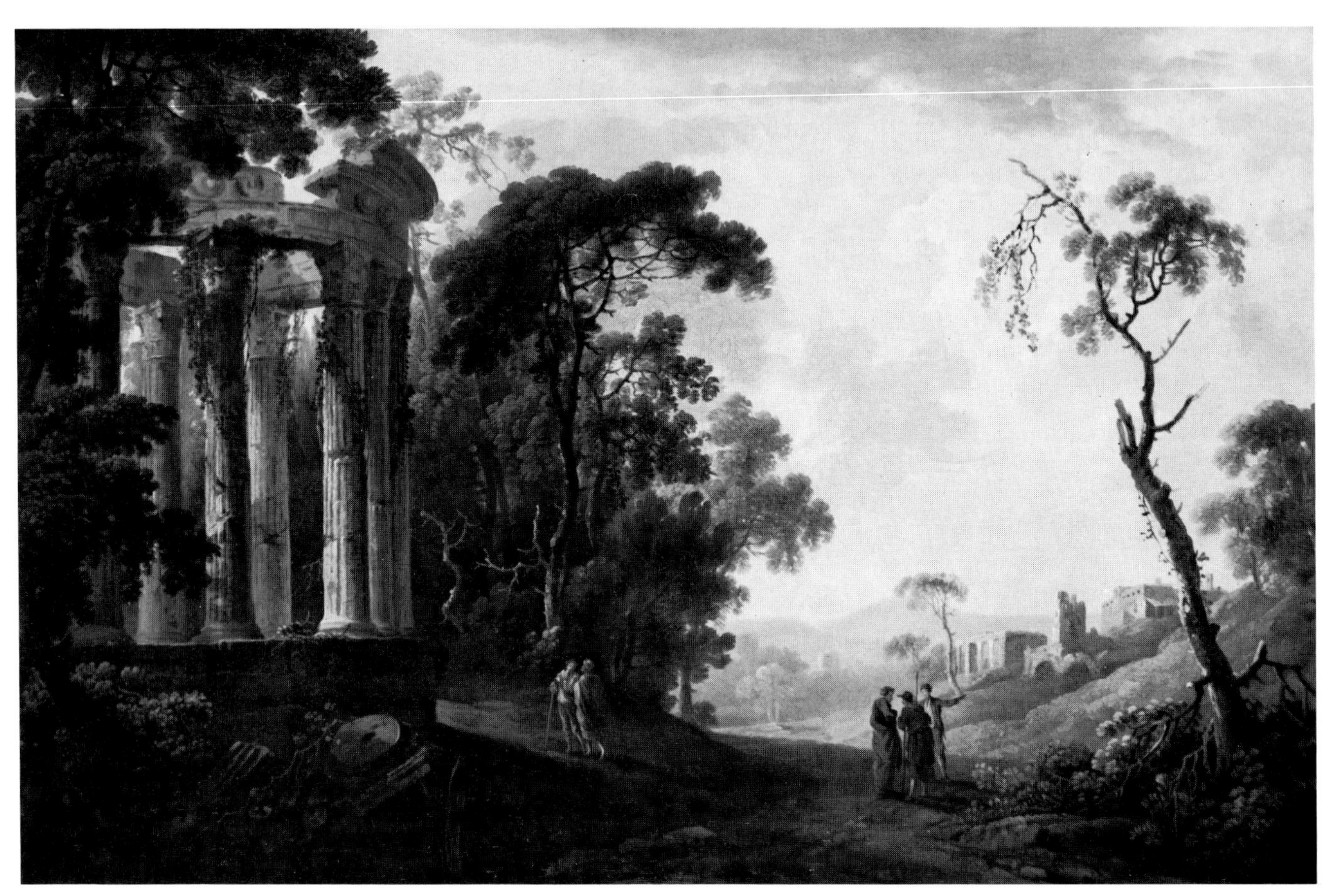

George Barret. *Landscape with Ruins*, ca. 1765 (no.3)

eyes.''[9] Clearly, though, DuFresnoy perceived ''Nature'' as the medium for an ideal form. The artist assembles the most beautiful aspects or elements of the visible world and, by purifying their qualities, creates an ideal form.

The aesthetic of the beautiful became a major theme of the *Discourses* (no. 7) Sir Joshua Reynolds (1732-92) delivered to the Royal Academy during his tenure as its first president, 1769-90. Reynolds, who had provided annotations for William Mason's 1783 translation of DuFresnoy, preserved the traditional perception of beauty as an ideal derived from nature and past masters. In his discussions, Reynolds distinguished between ''particular'' forms and ''generalized'' forms, or ''common'' from ''ideal'' nature. He expanded upon previous theories of the beautiful by outlining a plan for the artist's education. Having mastered the techniques of his medium, the artist must first imitate the appearance of ''particular'' nature through close observation and study of the human figure and the world. Next, the artist must study the achievements of past masters of the ideal.

> Study as nearly as you can, in the order, in the manner and on the principles on which they studied. Study nature attentively, but always with those masters in your company; consider them as models which you are to imitate, and at the same time as rivals with whom you are to contend. (Discourse VI, 1774)[10]

The result of this study of nature and past artists is the imitation of ''general nature.'' The artist now makes his subject the idea of beauty manifest in natural forms: ''This idea of the perfect state of nature, which the Artist calls Ideal Beauty, is the great leading principle by which works of genius are conducted...'' (Discourse III, 1770)[11].

These 18th-century academic principles put landscape in a relatively low position within the hierarchy of approved subject matter. For Reynolds and his successor, Benjamin West, the most important and noble pursuit of the artist was the painting of historical, allegorical, and religious subjects. Landscape fell behind history painting and even portraiture because it did not concentrate on human narrative or allegory to convey lofty themes. Some 17th-century landscape painters, however, idealized nature to express elevated moral statements. These artists were influential in the entire development of English landscape painting: Claude Lorrain (1600-82) and Gaspard Dughet (1615-75).[12] As Richard Wilson noted, their contributions to his painting were ''Claude for air and Gaspard for composition and sentiment.''[13] This statement is the keynote of British landscape painting in the classical tradition as Wilson exemplified it.

The 18th century regarded Claude Lorrain and Gaspard Dughet as models for the ideal in landscape compositions. Both French artists spent most of their lives in Italy forging links between the Italian landscape and the ideals of French aesthetics, as exemplified in the writings of their contemporary, DuFresnoy. Of Claude, Joshua Reynolds wrote, ''His pictures are a composition of the drafts which he had previously made from various beautiful scenes and prospects.'' (Discourse IV, 1771).[14] The landscape settings for Claude's allegorical and mythical subjects combine elements of actual Italian scenery in an orderly, balanced, and harmonious design, imposing a mood of undisturbed calm. One of Claude's characteristic formulas, constantly re-used by British and American painters, consists of a stage-like foreground bearing figures, a broad middle distance with a body of water, arched bridge, or a range of hills, and a light-struck background. A prominent tree enframes the view into the distance directed by a series of diagonal movements through space to the bright golden light on the horizon. Light serves as the unifying element in Claude's work, and a 1796 writer in *The New-York Weekly Magazine* remarked that ''we hardly behold a composition from his hand in which the rising or setting sun does not irradiate or warm his scenes.''[15] In contrast to Claude, Gaspard preferred wilder aspects of Italian scenery, such as the cascade and rocky terrain of Tivoli. Gaspard often composed his landscapes with a set of parallel planes or overlapping masses that recede into the distance through diminishing scale. His landscape spaces and forms have a greater sense of solidity and volume than Claude's do. Wilson's *Tivoli* closely follows Gaspard in its arrangement of a cloud-filled sky, elegantly attenuated tree, and buildings amassed on the Italian hills.

Although the British aristocracy had been collecting works of the classical landscape painters since the late 17th century, increased travel to Europe following the Peace of Utrecht in 1715 dramatically increased the vogue for Italian art. The grand tour became an essential aspect of every gentleman's education. For young artists, authors, and aristocrats, the tour culminated years of preparation for entry into elite society. After several years of war on the continent, Europe was opened for a flurry of British travellers who flocked to Italy in the 1750s. From this travel developed a resurgence of Italianate and classical influences in Britain during the 1760s. Richard Wilson's reputation crested in this decade when he established an honored position in British art for ideal landscape painting. However, the beautiful mode fell out of favor in Britain in the 1770s, although beautiful landscapes were produced well into the 19th century by such artists as Turner (nos. 4 & 5).

THE PICTURESQUE

It is notable that two of Lord Shelburne's three commissions during this decade of classical revival were of the people and scenery of Britain. Although the grand tour increased interest in continental scenery, other artists and authors began to consider the aesthetic potential of the British landscape. The first painters of British scenery were immigrant and touring artists from the continent, particularly Dutch and Flemish painters in the 17th and early 18th century. The close political relationship between the Dutch and English promoted cultural ties and an influx of 17th-century Dutch landscape paintings into the English art market in the 1740s. The example of Dutch views of domestic scenery inspired certain British artists to emulate their approach.

The Dutch landscape tradition deeply moved the first great English painter of the native landscape, Thomas Gainsborough. As a youth, Gainsborough displayed a proclivity for the pencil which led him to sketch his native Sud-bury after school. Intimate with the rural countryside, Gainsborough was naturally attracted to the Dutch landscapes of Jacob van Ruisdael (1628-82) and Meindert Hobbema (1638-1709), which were becoming popular in London when he arrived in 1740. Apprenticed to a French engraver, he also became versed in the French rococo. These two styles constantly inspired Gainsborough throughout his artistic career. The *View in Suffolk,* ca. 1755 (no. 14), is a masterpiece of the artist's early period in its synthesis of Dutch and French elements and its poetic approach to rural scenery. The horse with rider stops to drink at the river beside a dirt path that gently meanders past a pair of rustic lovers. Up the hillock the path leads to a farmer's cottage and curves into the distance. The rough, decayed trunk of the fallen tree and cottage nestled in the woods reflect the Dutch influences. The charming rustics courting in the foreground and the serpentine curve of the composition indicate Gainsborough's awareness of the French rococo. Yet the landscape is wholly English, evoking the gentle hills, sandy banks, and winding rivers of Suffolk. The mood of quaint rusticity and the natural details mark the beginning of a romantically passionate interest among English landscape painters in their distinctive native scenery.

The "nature" poets had preceded the painters in proclaiming the pictorial potential of the British landscape. Foremost among these authors was James Thomson (1700-48), whose monumental celebration of nature, *The Seasons* (London: 1726-30), is a landmark of English literature for its concentrated attention to nature. The poem was a departure from literary tradition in its descriptive realism and human perspective of nature as the vehicle for poetic mood. Previous literature had rarely utilized landscape as a metaphor for ideas and emotions. In *The Seasons* the poet directly reacts to nature, observing and describing scenes as a succession of pictures: "Till in the western sky the downward sun/Looks out effulgent-The rapid radiance instantaneous strikes/The illumin'd mountains-in a yellow mist/Bestriding earth-the grand ethereal bow/Shoots up immense, and every hue unfolds."[16] In addition, Thomson believed in a harmonious co-existence of man and nature that, as he noted in his preface

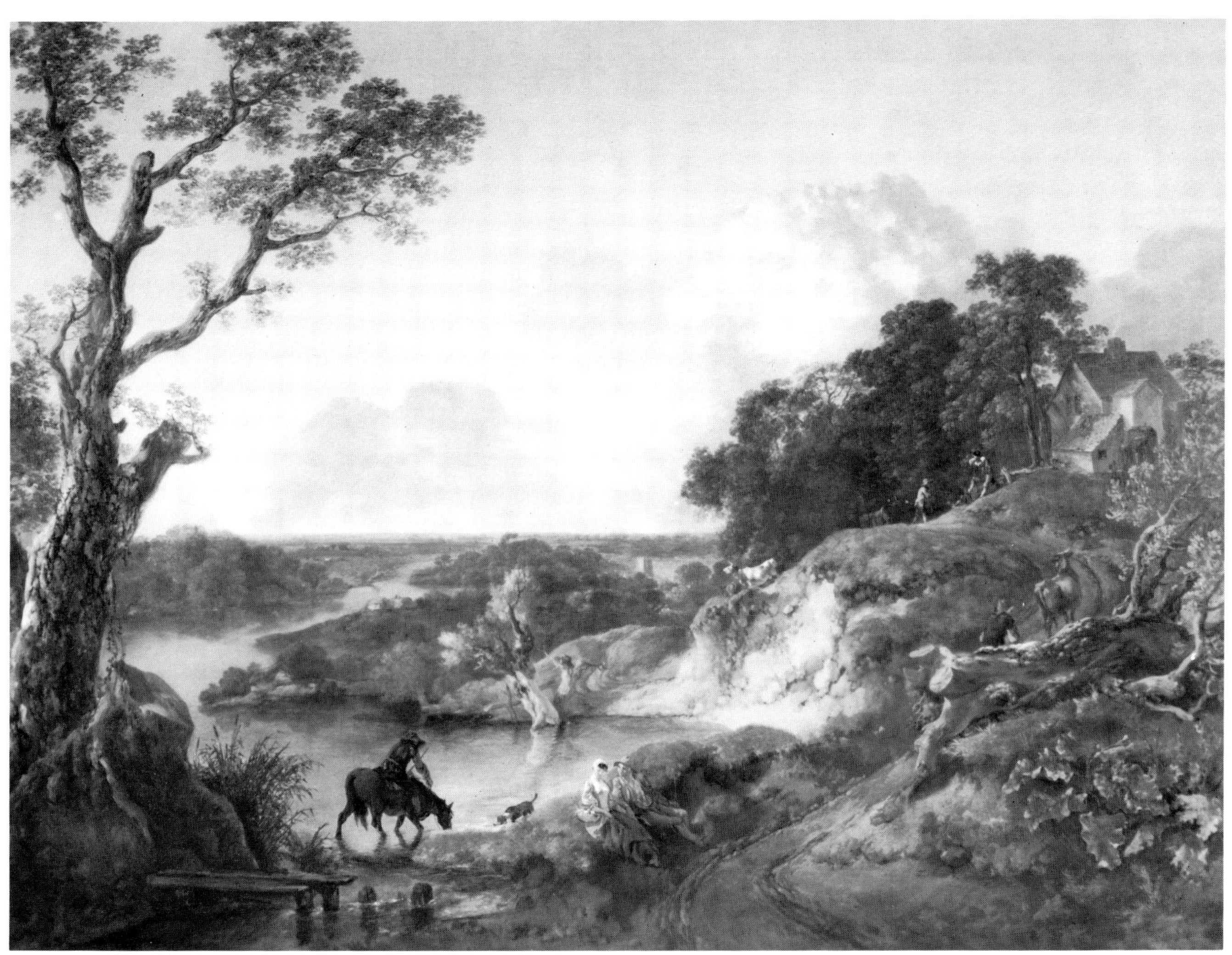

Thomas Gainsborough. *View in Suffolk*, ca. 1755 (no.14)

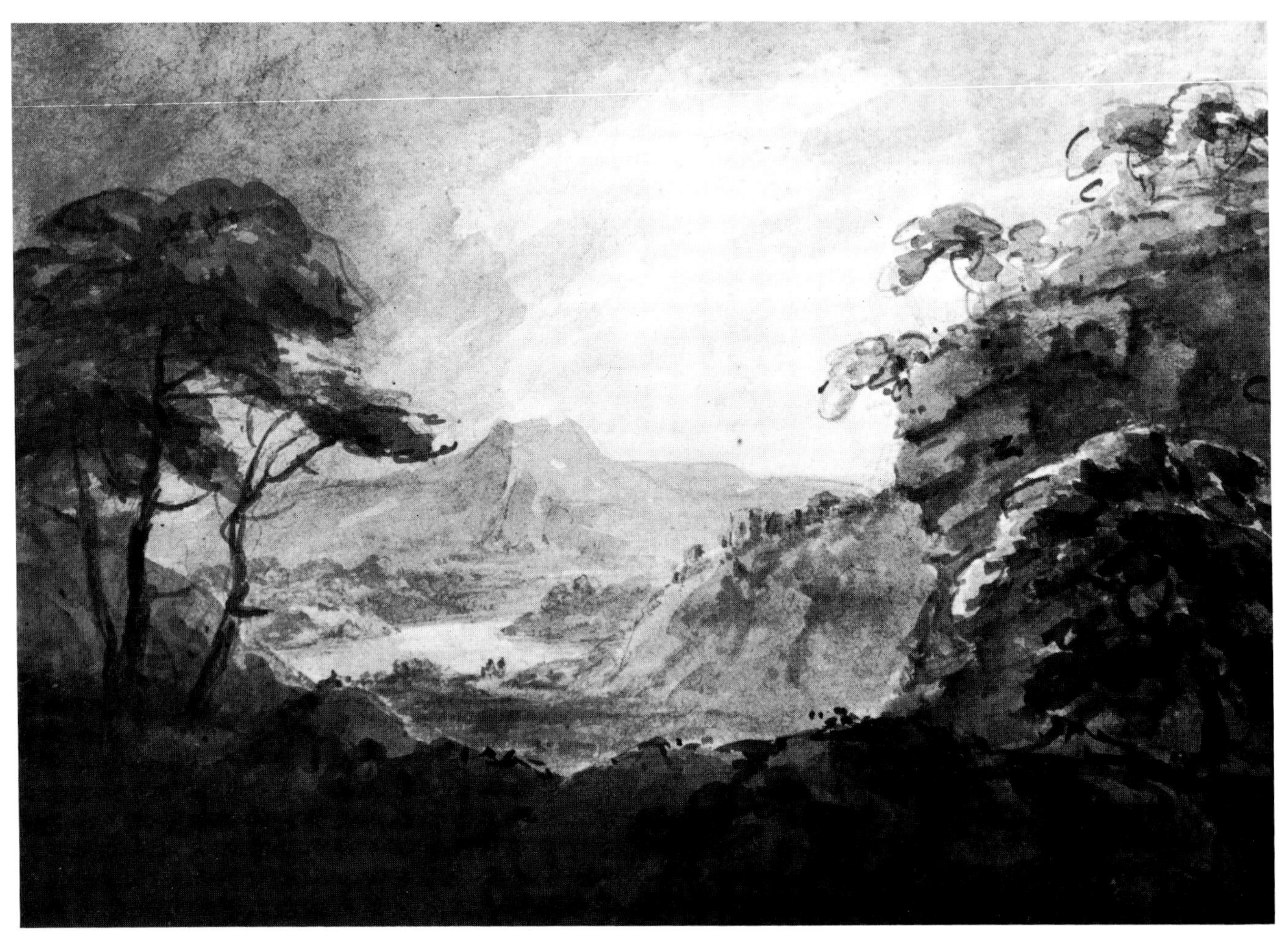

William Gilpin. *Landscape with River Valley* (no.17)

to *Winter,* gave cause for "philosophical reflection" and "moral sentiment."[17] Andrew Wilton highlights the significance of this poem when he notes, "Without the definitive success of Thomson's *Seasons* in the first half of the century, the development of landscape painting in England would have been rather different and perhaps delayed."[18]

Although the works of artists and writers such as Thomas Gainsborough and James Thomson partially account for the increasing popularity of native scenery in the late 18th century, this romantic phenomenon was more directly related to the fashion of touring picturesque scenery in England, Wales, and Scotland. Tour literature focusing on the Peak District, Lake District, and the Scottish highlands began to flourish in the 1770s. William Gilpin (1724-1804), in his influential tour books, beginning with *Observations on the River Wye* (1783, no. 18), elaborated the "picturesque" into a set of qualities that makes certain objects and scenes in nature "look well in a picture." The most important characteristic was roughness of texture, which can be distinguished from smoothness, the corresponding trait in the beautiful. All other qualities followed upon roughness: irregularity and variety, strong contrasts of light and shadow, novelty, and the capacity to affect the imagination. In his drawings, such as *Landscape with River Valley* (no. 17), Gilpin illustrates his formulas for picturesque landscape compositions. The rough, shadowy foreground is the stage for artistic license in effects of texture, color, and expression. The lighter middle-ground carries the "leading subject," a ruin on a sun-struck hill, that acts as the tonal center for the effects of light and shadow. The background sky and mountain range is the lightest, most indistinct region. Diagonal lines lead the eye naturally into the distance.

Gilpin's formulas and conventions are, in a general sense, variations on classical landscape compositions. The essential difference between a beautiful and a Gilpin landscape is one of mood. While the classical landscape has idealized and generalized forms that recede smoothly into the distance, the picturesque scene revels in vibrant silhouettes and rough textures. The mood is not one of idyllic repose, but rather of a stimulated attention to wild, uncultivated landscape. A native

of the rugged land in northern England, Gilpin was especially attracted to the Lake District, where the mixture of "the rural" and "the grand" made it, in his eyes, the most picturesque locale in Britain.

The many travellers, artists, and aestheticians combing the countryside in search of the picturesque greatly relished the excitement of exploring and drawing popular tour sites. Gilpin's writings inspired many to explore the remote edges of Britain and instigated a continuous debate on aesthetic tastes. His influence on British artists, however, is difficult to assess. As opposed to Gilpin's formulaic conventions for picturesque compositions, Thomas Gainsborough's picturesque scenes are composed with a rococo ambience that focuses on intimate, anecdotal incidents. Gainsborough and the successors to his style found infinite delight in sentimental depictions of rural life, whereas Gilpin believed that anecdotes interfered with an appreciation for picturesque scenery.

Paul Sandby's (1730-1809) tinted drawing, a fine example of his subtle tonal washes, employs a number of Gilpin's picturesque conventions (no. 15). The craggy tree casts a dark shadow over the foreground and enframes a view onto sunlit hills crested with a medieval tower. Its formal qualities and aesthetic temperament endorse Gilpin's ideas on the picturesque. For the most part, however, artists were less reliant on a specific application of Gilpin's theories. Philip J. de Loutherbourg's (1740-1812) *Wooded Landscape with Figures* (no. 16) is eminently picturesque for its lush, verdant forest interior enlivened by amorous rustics. The dense woods, peasants, and winding path recall Gainsborough's early style in the *View in Suffolk* (no. 14). De Loutherbourg painted many bucolic scenes in the early manner of Gainsborough, although he was primarily known for his dramatic shipwrecks and history paintings. Interestingly, the two artists were friends and may have toured the Lake District together in 1783. If not, they certainly knew each other's work, establishing a direct link in this branch of English rural landscape painting.

The picturesque lived on into the first two decades of the 19th century as a viable aesthetic around which debate was active. Aside from the theories and artistic conventions it

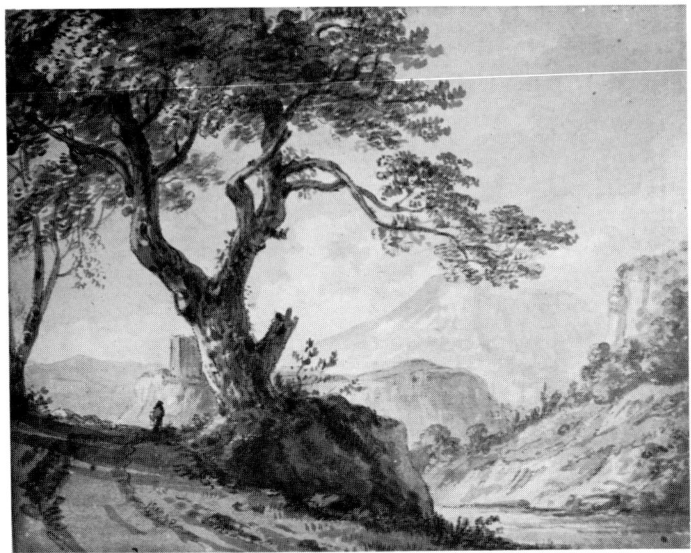

Paul Sandby. *Landscape with Tree, Tower and Mountain,*
ca. 1790 (no.15)

generated, the picturesque made its most important contribution to British culture by promoting a concentrated examination of and genuine enthusiasm for native landscape. Early picturesque writers and painters composed landscapes into artificially "natural" designs. After the turn of the 19th century, a group of younger artists transformed the conventions and artifice of picturesque landscape painting by approaching familiar English farm and mill country with an eye for objective details of light, atmosphere, and texture. Rather than regarding the rugged elements of British scenery as picturesque, they emphasized the inherent variety and visual appeal of more settled, domesticated landscapes. Many of these artists, such as John Crome (1768-1821) in Norwich and John Constable (1776-1837) in Suffolk, adopted a section of the country as their painting terrain. These young artists painted only the areas of England with which they were intimately familiar. Constable accurately summarized this attitude when

he wrote that "I shall endeavor to get a pure and unaffected manner of representing the scenes that may employ me. . . There is room enough for a natural painture."[19] This sentiment, widespread among the young generation of artists around London, in East Anglia, and in other sections of England, has led John Gage to label the 1810s the "decade of Naturalism."[20]

The ideas of one picturesque theorist, Sir Uvedale Price (1747-1829), are directly relevant to this development in English landscape painting. In his *Essay on the Picturesque* (1794, no. 24), Price, as had Gilpin, approached nature as it approximated the effects of painting. Unlike Gilpin, Price was especially attracted to rural, rather than wild scenery, and he took great pains to determine the relative picturesqueness of cottages, rolling hills, farms, laborers, animals, and the works of past artists. A childhood friend of Gainsborough, Price was probably inspired by the painter to see in rural England and the Dutch masters the qualities of the picturesque.

Although Crome and the other artists of the regional Norwich School held no pretensions to picturesque theorizing, they wholeheartedly embraced in their paintings the Norfolk heaths, the Yarmouth shore, and the rivers of southeast England with an eye for picturesque contrast and variety. On the title page of the 1816 exhibition catalog, the Norwich Society of Artists proclaimed, "Examine first when Truth and Taste decree, / What Nature is, Painting ought to be."[21] Because John Crome was the chief organizer of that group, his paintings are the ultimate manifestations of the Norwich aesthetic. The *Landscape,* ca. 1809 (no. 22), from Crome's middle years, probably depicts some familiar spot on the Wensum or Yare rivers the artist cherished for its intimate seclusion. Two youths quietly play on the river bank, while across the water two trees echo them in prominent silhouettes against the sky. The dark, warm browns and greens of the land contrast to the cool blue sky. The image of a benevolent nature in harmony with man, the pictorial effects of contrast in tonal value, and the varied silhouettes signal Crome's relation to the picturesque traditions of both Gainsborough and Gilpin.

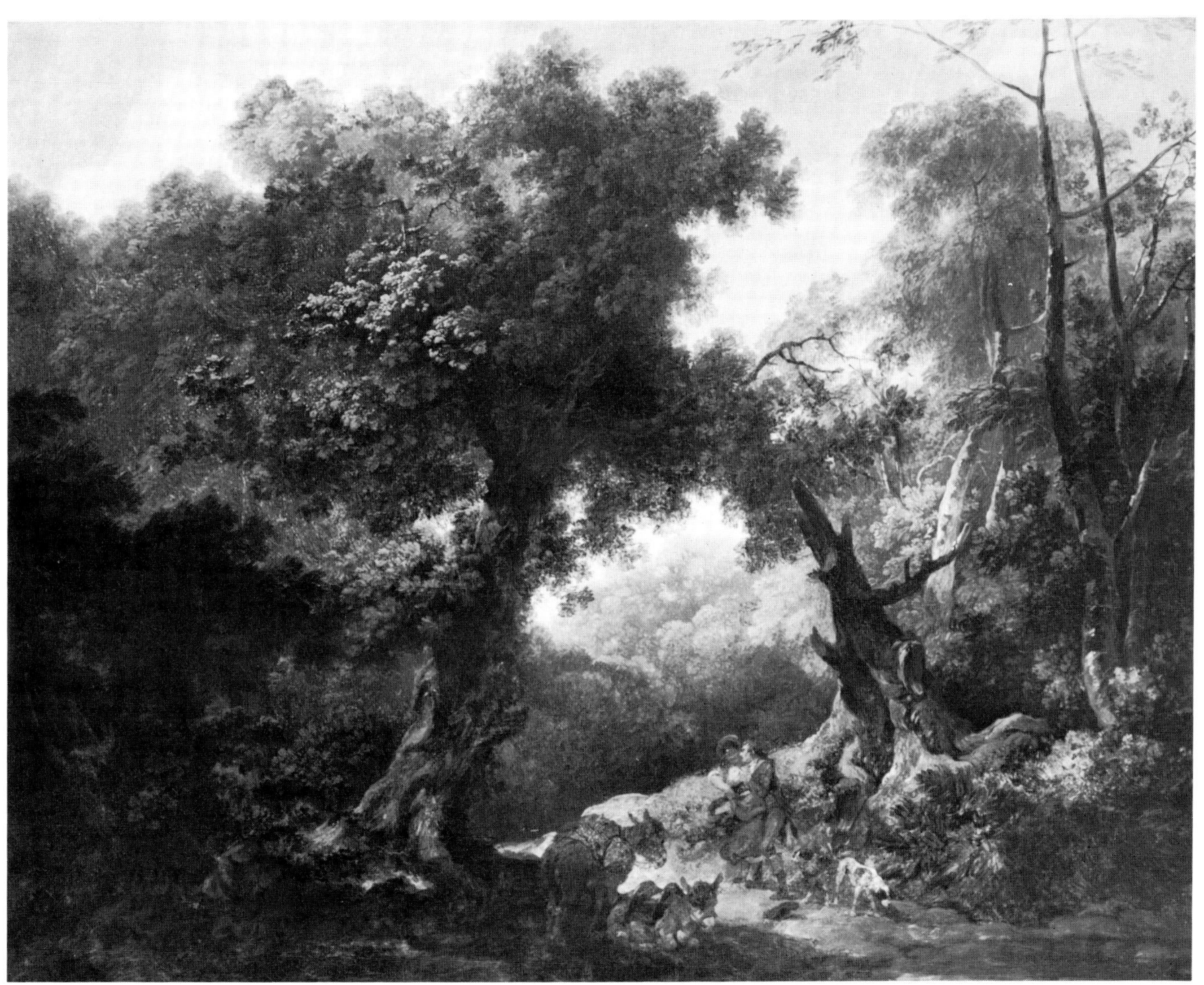

Philip J. de Loutherbourg. *Wooded Landscape with Figures* (no.16)

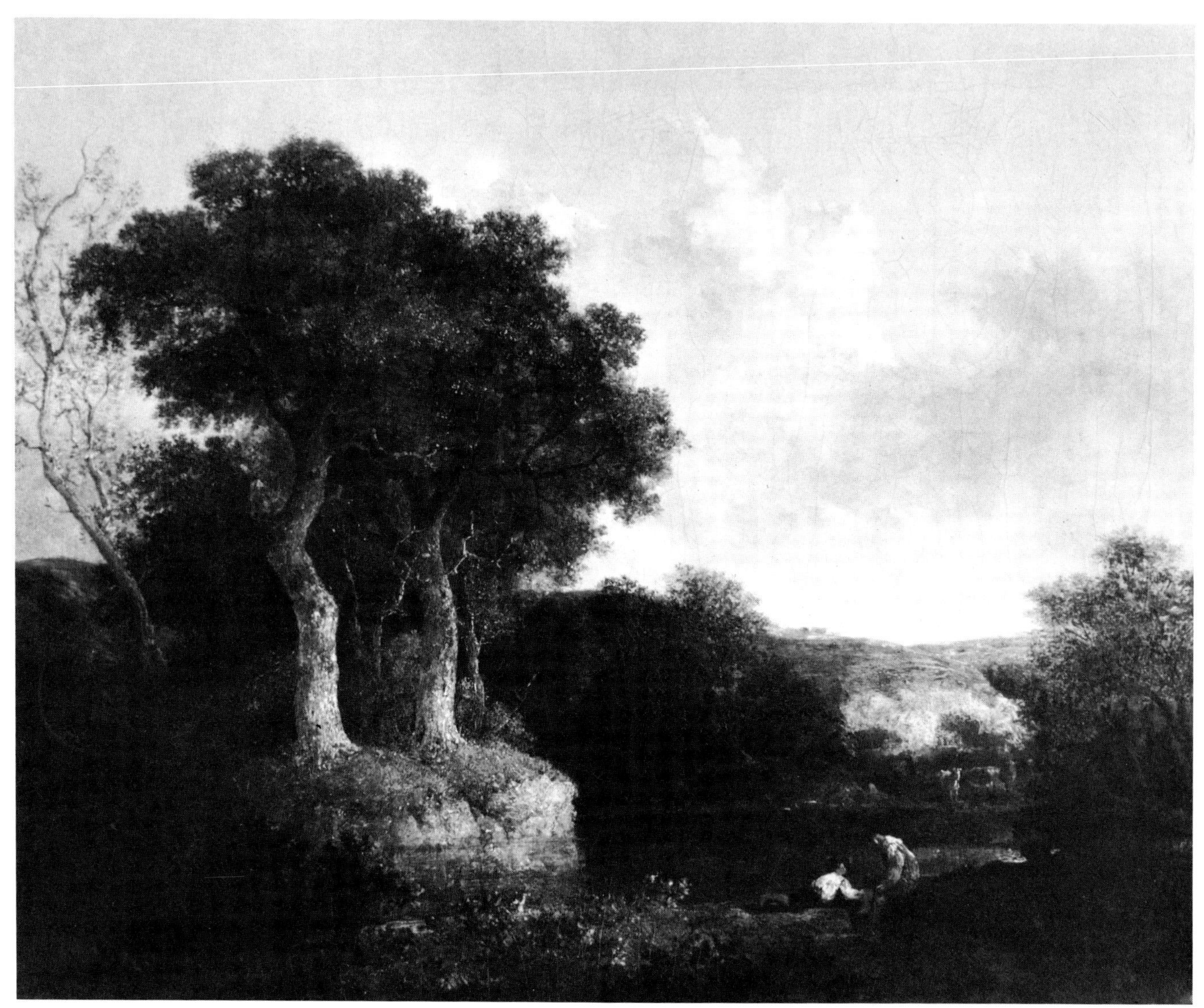

John Crome. *Landscape*, ca. 1809 (no.22)

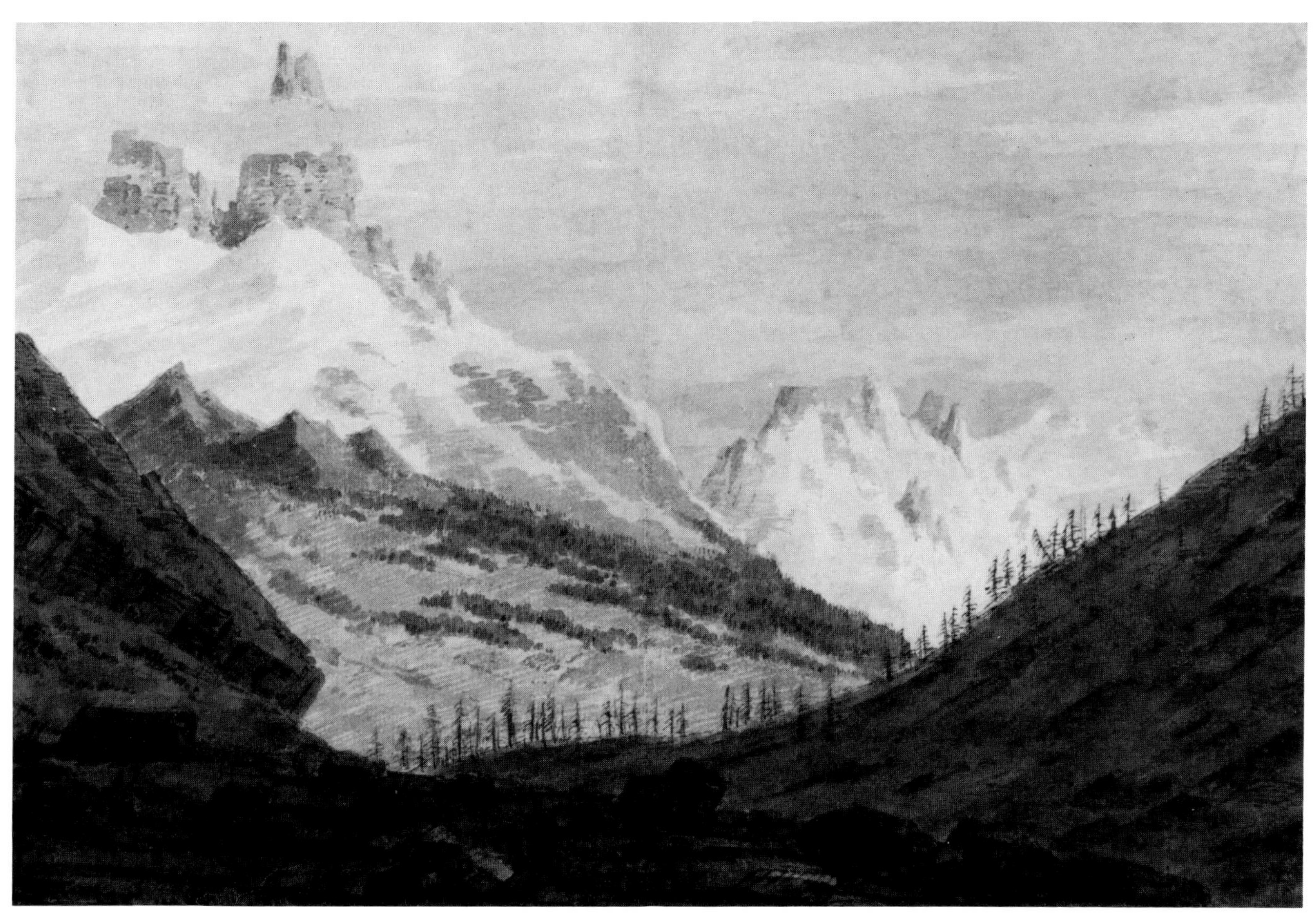

John Robert Cozens. *Between Chamonix and Martigny*, 1776 (no.36)

The Sublime

A third category of aesthetic response to landscape drew upon the long literary tradition of the sublime, and in 18th-century art and aesthetics, the ''sublime'' came to be associated with spiritually and emotionally exciting elements of nature. The sublime was also the most radical, romantic development in 18th-century British art. While the beautiful landscape evokes a pastoral ideal and the picturesque introduces rustic, familiar scenes, the sublime ''lift[s] up the soul; to exalt it into ecstacy.''[22] In the visual arts this excited approach to the awesome in nature led to a new genre of mountainscapes. Mountains were rare subjects in western art and literature before the Age of Enlightenment, when they were viewed as dangerous barriers and remnants of the diluvian age. Not until the early 18th century did travellers and philosophers acknowledge and appreciate the grandeur of mountain scenery. Several scholars attribute this change in attitude to a revision in religious interpretations of mountains.[23] As early as the 17th century, the liturgical theorist Thomas Burnet wrote of the exciting mixture of attraction and repulsion in the presence of vast mountains. ''Whatsoever hath the Shadow and Appearance of the Infinite'' fills the mind with wonder and great thoughts. ''We do naturally, upon such Occasions, think of God and his Greatness.''[24] This conceptual leap from dread and loathing to a religious awe of mountains opened the door to an aesthetic appreciation of mountain majesty.

As in the case of the interest in picturesque landscape, the writers and philosophers of the sublime preceded the artists. Travellers touring Europe in the 18th century wrestled with conflicting feelings of fear and exaltation when confronted by the Swiss Alps. Thomas Gray's reaction to the Alps in 1739 reveals his awareness of the dangers surrounding him and the metaphorical implications of infinity and grandeur: ''There are certain scenes that would awe an atheist into belief, without the help of other argument.''[25] An active appreciation of the sublime in mountains did not occur among visual artists until the fourth quarter of the 18th century. Although many draftsmen had accompanied gentlemen through the Alps on their grand tours earlier in the century, their pictures were tame, safe views, removed from the terror and exaltation actually experienced.

No artist captured these qualities before John Robert Cozens (1752-97) made his first grand tour in 1776. He apparently made no sketches until he reached Switzerland, the first dramatic scenery on the long journey to Italy. One sketch, inscribed and dated on the back ''Between Chamouny & Martinach / August 30 1776'' (no. 36),[26] documents Cozens' direct encounter with the steep rise of the snow-capped Alps piercing the clouds. Cozens concentrates on the sharp diagonal rise of the mountainsides to create an impression of infinity in the mountains. An absence of human figures does not allow a moment's relief from this awesome site just at the timberline and verging upon a desolation of rock and ice. The viewer is forced to confront nature in its most awesome state. The trail to the precipice in the distance is entirely cut off and, visually, impassible by man. There are few earlier landscapes that offer such a formidable view.

Travel literature of the day also inspired certain artists to explore the sublime potential of native landscapes. Derwentwater, a popular tour stop in the Lake District, provided many artists with picturesque material for paintings. Joseph Wright of Derby (1734-97) found at Derwentwater a harsh, volatile landscape of fierce beauty and violent change. Wright held a special affection for the mountains of his native Peak District, which he often painted. Later in life Wright ventured into the Lake District (1793 and 1794) and discovered new subjects for his landscapes. Of his extant views of the lakes, the 1795-96 *Derwentwater, with Skiddaw in the Distance* (no. 37) is one of the most dynamic and impressive.[27] The vast panorama of lake and mountain is dramatic for its energetic sky, charged with rain and swiftly-moving clouds. The miniscule figures gazing into the landscape emphasize the immense scale of the mountains and, conversely, the insignificance of man in the face of nature's omnipotence.

These visual renderings of sublime imagery bear many formal correspondences with the controversial theory of Edmund Burke (1729-97), expounded in *A Philosophical Inquiry*

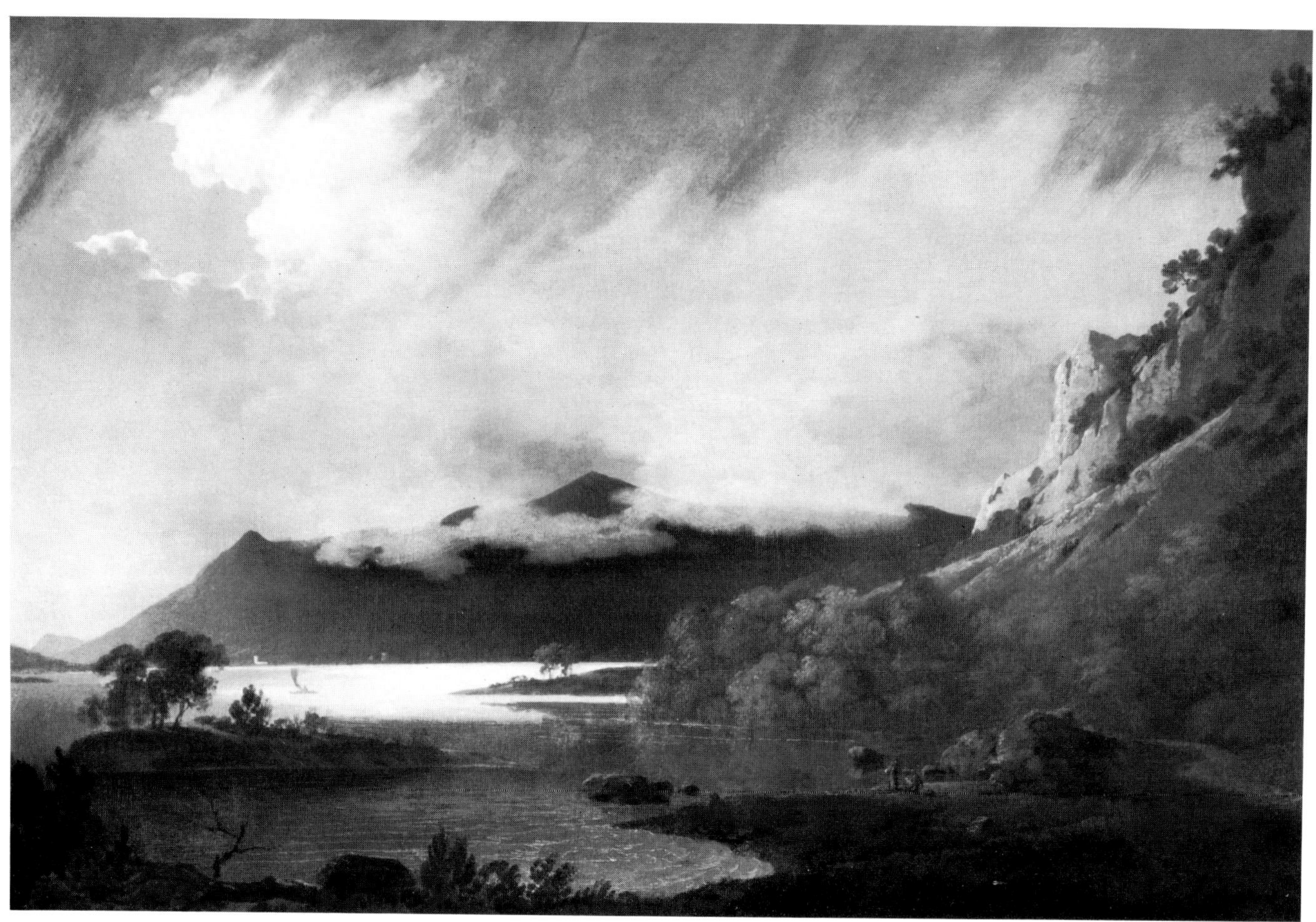

Joseph Wright of Derby. *Derwentwater, with Skiddaw in the Distance*, 1795-96 (no.37)

into the Origins of our Ideas of the Sublime and Beautiful, (1757, no. 43). Specific relations between his writings and late 18th-century paintings are tenuous; the theory, however, does provide a framework for understanding the contemporary usage of the term "sublime." Burke believed that sublime feelings involve awe, astonishment, and enlargement of soul, and are triggered by immensity, grandeur, and danger. "Whatever is fitted in any sort to excite the ideas of pain and danger, that is to say, whatever is in any sort terrible, or is conversant about terrible objects...is a source of the sublime."[28] Once the viewer is safe from actual danger or pain, he may experience aesthetic pleasure, what Burke termed "a sort of delightful horror, a sort of tranquility tinged with terror."[29] Though Burke did not specifically link the sublime with landscape, a close follower, Hugh Blair, in *Lectures on Rhetoric and Belles Lettres* (1783), made the connection clear: "What are the scenes of nature that elevate the mind in the highest degree, and produce the sublimest sensation? Not the gay landscape, the flowery field, or the flourishing city, but the hoary mountain, and the solitary lake; the aged forest, and the torrent falling over the rock."[30]

The sublimity of mountain imagery reached its pinnacle in the works of Joseph M.W. Turner (1775-1851). Probably the most prolific British painter of mountains, Turner staged dramas of men pitted against the elements. After the cessation of two decades of French hostilities in 1802, Turner quickly traveled to Switzerland, making dozens of sketches of mountain scenes. Though three summers of travel through North Wales and northern England had conditioned him for mountain scenery, he was overwhelmed by the immensity of the Alps. Immediately upon his return and over the next decade, Turner painted a series of magnificent watercolors of Swiss scenery. The spectacle of the tiny shepherds leading their flock to cover from the fast approaching storm is only an anecdotal incident in *Chamonix,* ca. 1809 (no. 38). The real drama lies in the steep incline of the rugged mountainside, the precarious viewpoint and the forbidding storm that envelops the view. Nature, in its raw and primal state, is the source of terror in this picture. The dominant axis is the diagonal climbing across the picture surface, a marked contrast to the balanced, classical composition by Richard Wilson (no. 1). In addition, the bold contrasts of warm and cool blue washes heightened the drama for an early 19th-century viewer conditioned to golden brown paintings with tonal gradations. These formal qualities, in concert with the forceful sweep of the mountainside and clouds, are the pictorial equivalent of Burke's qualities of the sublime: immensity, grandeur, and danger.

A century before Lord Shelburne's commission of landscapes by his countrymen, British landscape painting had been inaugurated by Dutch and Flemish artists, who brought their styles to the hitherto unpainted range of British landscape subjects. Later, Sir Joshua Reynolds established a strong British link to the idealist aesthetics of Charles DuFresnoy and other European classical theorists with his educational program at the Royal Academy. Successive collecting vogues for the works of the 17th-century continental landscape masters aided in the establishment of the ideal, classical style of British landscape painting. In conceiving of nature as raw material for painting, British artists gradually turned their interest to the mountains, moors, and farmlands of their own country. The inspiring grandness of the Swiss Alps provided the basis for a new style of sublime landscape, one readily adaptable to the awesome and majestic aspects of British scenery. Shortly after the death of Turner in 1851, the taste in British landscape painting shifted from the Italian idyll, the epic sublime, and the rustic picturesque towards an exacting realism inspired by Ruskin and the Pre-Raphaelites. The three categories of the beautiful, the sublime, and the picturesque had outlived their usefulness as aesthetic principles, but the history of their development mirrors the growth in Britain of a profound appreciation of British scenery.

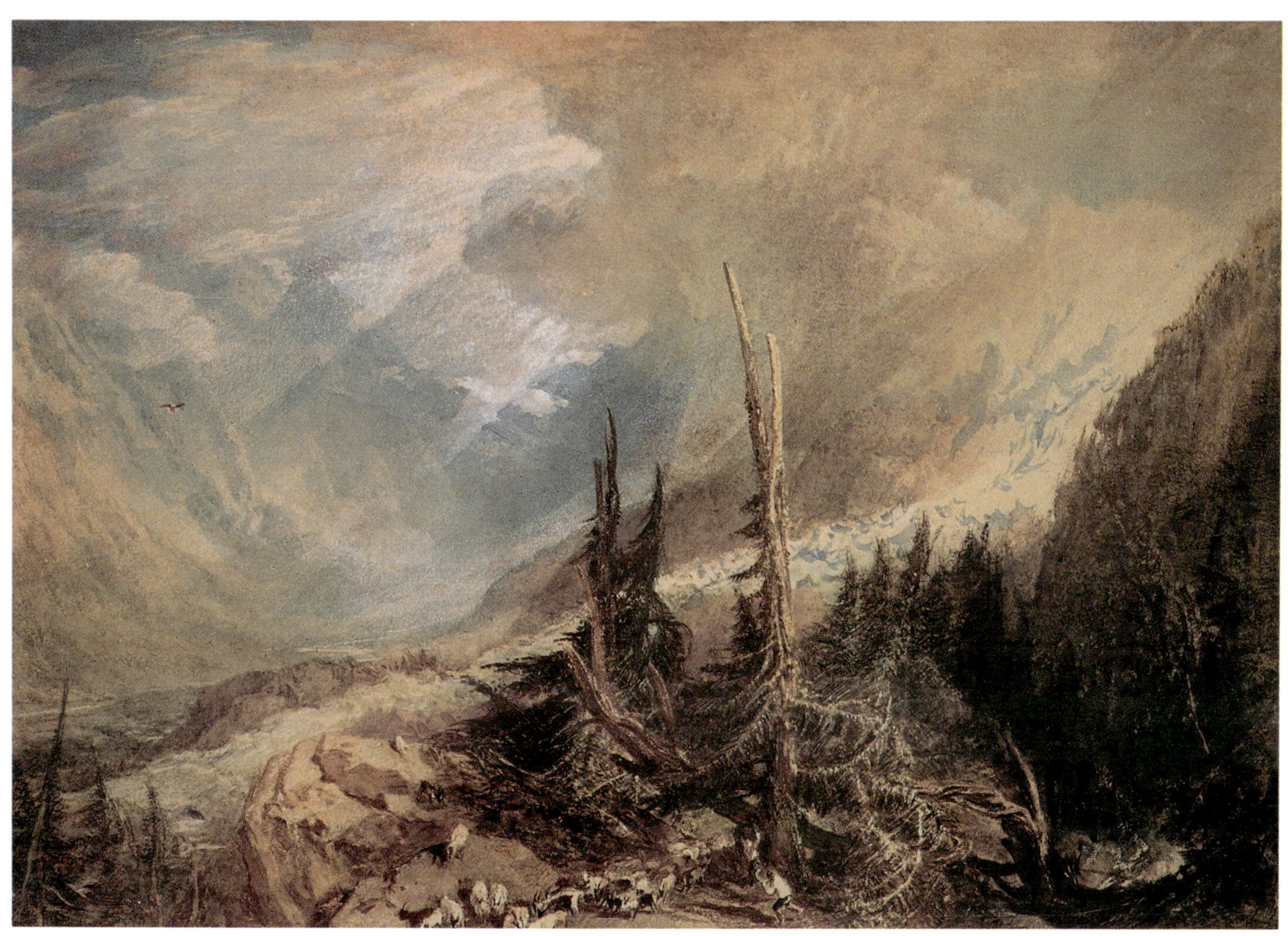

Joseph M.W. Turner. *Chamonix*, ca. 1809 (no.38)

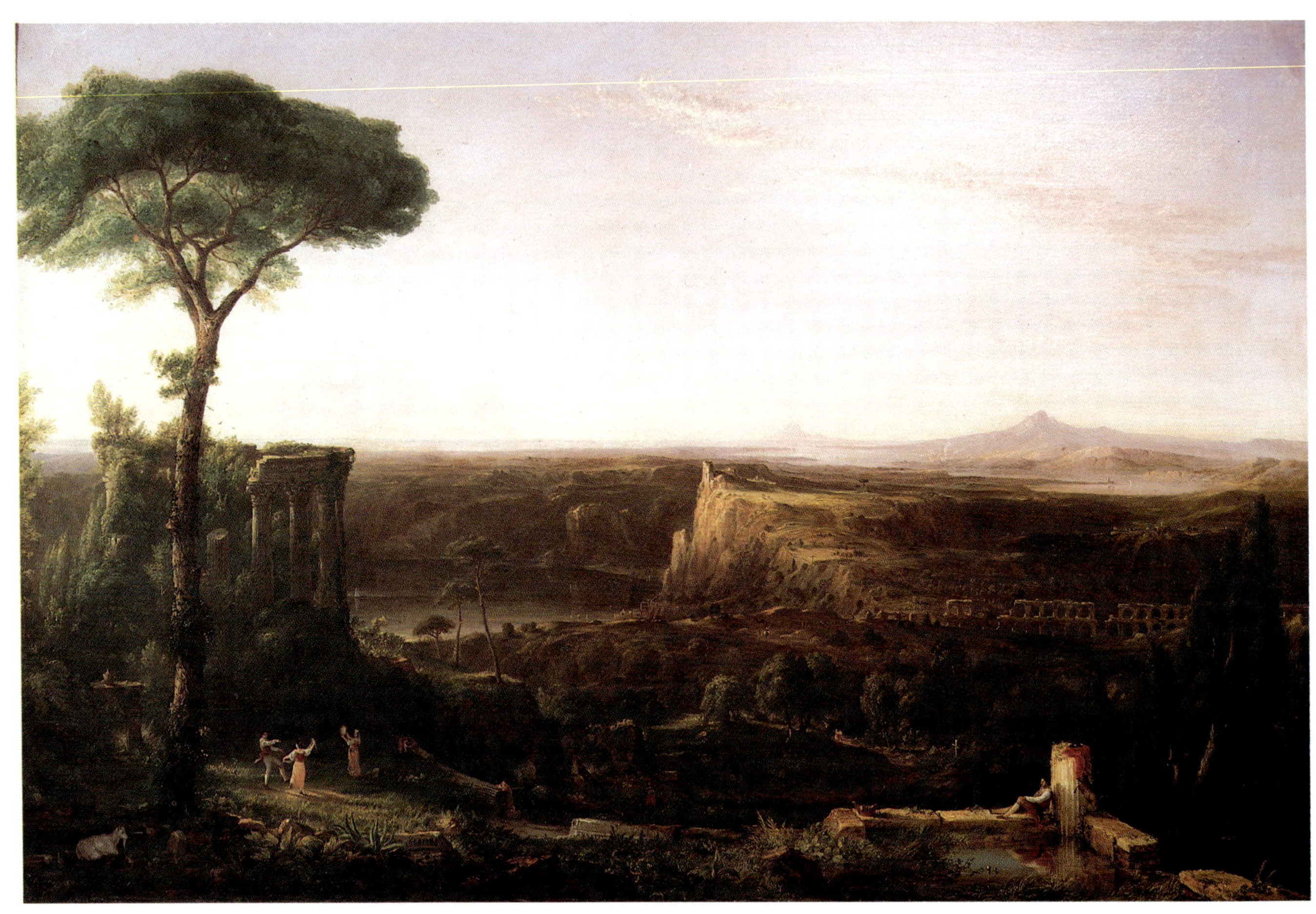

Thomas Cole. *Landscape Composition, Italian Scenery*, 1833 (no.9)

L ANDSCAPE PAINTING in America evolved along similar, if not parallel, lines of development to those in Britain. The earliest efforts in rendering American scenery were based on British aesthetic models, a natural development insofar as descendants of British colonists largely populated the new nation. In surveying the first century of landscape painting in this country, it is evident that Americans transformed the British modes of the beautiful, the sublime, and the picturesque to articulate their concerns and the unique character of their land. Just as the British dialogue with European traditions eventually led to a discovery of the aesthetic riches of the British landscape, so did American artists' use of British aesthetic conceptions and artistic formulas lead to a greater appreciation of the American landscape. By the middle of the 19th century, a body of like-minded artists, dubbed the Hudson River School, had firmly established landscape painting as a truly American specialty, capturing the imagination of the nation with their paintings of settled and wilderness America. By employing the formulas, subjects, and aesthetics of British landscape, American painters established a continuity of tradition from the Old World to the New. However, the vital concern for a unique cultural identity led American artists to alter the original parameters and objectives of the three British landscape modes. In American paintings and prints, these categories no longer bear such marked distinctions as in British art. One category in particular, the picturesque, was liberally applied to scenery British aestheticians would have deemed beautiful or sublime. In addition, certain American artists, such as Thomas Cole, Asher Durand, and Frederic Church, painted landscapes in all three modes or combined aspects of more than one tradition within a single painting. By separately analyzing the American versions of each mode, however, we can account for both similarities and disparities between British and American expressions of the beautiful, the picturesque, and the sublime.

The Hudson River painters expressed the first distinctively American vision of their native landscape. By the time of the first generation's debut as landscape painters in the 1820s and 30s, the aesthetic ideas of British landscape art had become well-known, and Americans had an awareness of the achievements of Turner and other British artists. The British influence reached America by four channels: British painters in America; American artists in Europe; American art institutions in imitation of the Royal Academy; and American reading of British books and journals.

Until the beginning of the 19th century, there were no professional landscape painters in America. Landscape art was an imported genre in America, and like the earliest manifestations of British landscape painting, it was mainly confined, before 1820, to the accurate portrayal of country estates and the proud young cities of the Eastern seaboard. Like the Dutch and Flemish artists who brought topographic painting to Britain in the late 17th century, the immigrant or visiting landscape painters were fully versed in the contemporary modes of their genre. The first group of Englishmen arrived in the 1790s and included the painters William Winstanley (fl. 1792-1806), William Groombridge (1748-1811), George Beck, (1748-1812), and Francis Guy (ca. 1760-1820). These artists painted American subjects in a topographic manner, but occasionally created landscapes that reveal their knowledge of contemporary sublime and picturesque conventions. A second generation of painters came in the 1810s, and among them was Joshua Shaw, who figured prominently in the development of American picturesque landscape painting.

The migration of British landscape painters to the unpainted wilds of America was reciprocated by Americans traveling to Europe for study and inspiration. Benjamin West (1738-1820), the American-born successor to Reynolds as leader of the Royal Academy, advanced this trans-atlantic exchange of artists. West had become one of Britain's leading history painters by the time he was elected the second president of the Academy in 1792. His own "Discourses" carried Reynolds' ideas into the next century, but with the important difference of urging the student to follow "that line and that expression of that art which the natural turn of his genius shall lead him to embrace."[31] This liberal philosophy allowed for landscape painting as a legitimate pursuit of the artist, and though West himself rarely painted landscapes, his direction of the Academy coincided with the emergence of a new generation of painters committed to landscape. In the early years of his administration, Philip de Loutherbourg, Thomas Hearne (no. 21), and Paul Sandby were among the Academy's exhibitors, and in the last decade of West's tenure, David Cox (no. 23), John Crome, J.M.W. Turner and John Constable were regularly presented.

West's generous hosting of American artists visiting Britain on the first leg of their European sojourns marked his strongest role in the transfer of British ideas to the New World. Partly in obedience to established European tradition, but mainly out of frustration with the limited opportunities for study and patronage in America, many American artists traveled to Europe shortly after the turn of the 19th century. In London they studied at the Royal Academy and in the great public collections and received the guidance of West, who was known widely for his friendliness to American students. He allowed the visiting artists access to his immense collection of European art and arranged for them to meet such celebrated landscape masters as Turner. Several artists who studied under West, notably Washington Allston (1779-1843), John Vanderlyn (1775-1852), and Samuel Morse (1791-1872), became specialists in history and portrait painting, but diversified their work with pure landscapes.

Although these pupils of West tended to regard landscape as only a sideline or private enterprise, they succeeded in conveying to other Americans a romantic enthusiasm for European scenery and the value of study abroad. Allston advocated a study trip to Europe in an 1827 letter outlining a course of study for the young Thomas Cole. Cole should spend at least half of his time in England: "The present English school comprises a great body of excellent artists and many eminent in every branch. At the head of. . .[Cole's] department he will find Turner, who 'take him all in all' has no superior of any age." Some time should be spent in France, and the rest of the trip should take in Italy's splendid land-

scape and wealth of classical art. "I should therefore recommend it to your friend to place at the head of his list Claude, Titian, the two Poussins, Salvator Rosa and Francesco Mola, together with Turner and the best of the modern artists."[32]

The works of English artists and past masters of European painting were known in America at this time chiefly through reproductive prints and illustrated British publications on art. Prints after the "old masters" were standard educational devices of the various American academies of art established in the early decades of the 19th century. Modelling themselves after the Royal Academy, these fledgling art institutions consequently brought to American art the idealist aesthetics of Joshua Reynolds, his belief in the moral purpose of art, and his emphasis on the study of past masters. For these institutions, history painting was the highest calling of the artist, and pure landscape could compete with historical or allegorical themes only if modelled after the landscapes of the 17th-century classicists. By promoting study of these past masters, through prints and travel to Europe, the early American art academies ensured the development of an American version of the pastoral, ideal landscape.

Some of the largest American private collections could boast English and Italian landscapes; Robert Gilmor, the Baltimore patron of Cole and Thomas Doughty, possessed "undoubtedly original" works by Nicolas Poussin, Salvator Rosa, George Barret, and Richard Wilson.[33] More readily accessible, however, were British treatises and art manuals, released in American editions or imported via a thriving transatlantic book trade. John Burnet's *Practical Treatise on Painting* (London: 1827) and other popular instruction books contained both detailed discussion of the European schools and illustrations of characteristic works. These British books helped to inspire an American fascination with the achievements of European painting. In backwoods Ohio about 1821-22, for example, "an English work on painting, illustrated with engravings, and treating of design, composition and color" inspired Thomas Cole. As his biographer, Louis Noble, relates, "A curtain suddenly rose, and exhibited to him a vision of renown. . .While the long train of old masters, Raphael, Titian, Claude, Salvator, passed before him like so many celestials, the names of modern artists sounded like titled heroes. His ambition and resolve to become a landscape painter were complete."[34]

THE BEAUTIFUL

As a founding-member of the National Academy of Design in New York, Thomas Cole (1801-48) adhered to the traditional academic conception of the purpose of art but was convinced from the beginning of his career that landscape could satisfy both moral and aesthetic ends. Cole was born in England and in 1818 emigrated with his family to America. He labored in obscurity in Ohio and Pennsylvania during the early 1820s, painting portraits and genre scenes while developing his skill as an interpreter of the native landscape. In New York in 1825, Cole was discovered by John Trumbull (1756-1843), a pupil of West and then the president of the American Academy of Fine Arts. Within a year the young artist was widely recognized as one of the foremost landscape painters in the country. Though he aspired to success as a painter of literary and allegorical landscapes, Cole most impressed his fellow Americans with forcefully realistic renditions of the unsettled wilderness. He realized that America's great uncharted tracts of wilderness made its landscape distinctly different from Old World scenery. To further his education, Cole studied in Europe from 1829 to 1832, roughly following the itinerary Allston had suggested. Cole's friends in New York were concerned that he not abandon his interest in the American wilderness. William Cullen Bryant's poem "To Cole, the Painter, Departing for Europe" urged the artist to "keep that earlier, wilder image bright," though his eyes will be drawn "to the light of distant skies."[35]

The National Gallery of London had some great works by Claude Lorrain, and Cole praised them for the "mellow melting and appropriate" touch, the "pearly cool tone" of the skies, and the beautiful gradations of light into shadow.[36] In Italy during 1831-32 Cole fell in love with the beauties of the landscape that had inspired the old masters. His appreciation and understanding of the classical painters were substan-

tially increased. Writing to William Dunlap after his return, Cole stated that "Claude, to me, is the greatest of all landscape painters."[37] This echoes the British sentiment that "of all the Landskip-Painters, Claude Lorrain has the most Beautiful and Pleasing ideas."[38]

Cole's admiration for Claude and his complex reaction to Italian landscape found expression in numerous Italian compositions that supplemented his better known wilderness subjects. Of these, the *Landscape Composition, Italian Scenery,* 1833 (no. 9), is one of the most ambitious, synthesizing actual and imaginary elements of Italian scenery. Reminiscent of Claude, the foreground is a stage leading to the panoramic middleground with a lake ringed by rounded hills. Far in the distance is the ethereal apparition of a mountain. A glowing sunny sky takes up fully half of this scene, a hallmark of the Italian classical landscape especially appealing to the Americans. A massive Italian pine connects the detailed foreground and the pristine sky, and acts as a framing element in concert with the trees rising up from beneath the ruins at right. Traces of the passage of time fill the tremendous expanse of space in the middleground: the weathered contours of the hills, a ruined aqueduct, a castle-like ruin overlooking the still lake. In the foreground, broken architectural fragments litter the lush carpet of vegetation; a circular temple at left, suggesting the Temple of the Sibyl at Tivoli, is returning to the earth as foliage overwhelms it. Wilson painted a more accurate portrayal of the ruined temple in his mid-1760s composition of *Tivoli* (no. 1), situating it on a distant bluff against a backdrop of clouds. By contrast, Cole brought the temple to the foreground and placed it opposite the angular, eroded cliff above the lake as a symbol of nature's triumph over civilization.

The Italian landscape offered Cole and other American painters the opportunity to consider the mutability of life and the passage of civilizations. For Richard Wilson, the classical painters and the Italianate landscape offered the style and subjects of a timeless ideal, an approach to perfect nature. American landscape painters emphasized the aesthetic qualities of Italian scenery that appealed to the British classicists, the golden light, varied, rich terrain, and soft atmosphere. Cole utilized the Claudian format as a framework for presenting the ancient landscape's moral lessons. The contrasting figures of *Italian Scenery*'s foreground are reflections of Cole's conflicting responses to Italy. At left, a group of dancing peasants celebrate the beauty of the scenery, while at right, a lone figure, seated at the base of a ruined column, broods over the landscape. Noble imagined Cole's reaction to the ancient Italian hills and their crumbling ruins: "He saw himself on the seashore of history, and the wrecks of human passion, pride, ambition, joy and sorrow, pricking through its sands."[39]

The use of classical compositions demonstrated that the ideals of the classical landscape were alive in present day America. The use of Claudian conventions for American scenery endowed the American landscape with a historical respectability. Barbara Novak has written on the attraction of the Claudian format:

> On it could be loaded all the connotations of Ambition, of competition with European culture, that American artists not so secretly harbored. It offered the artists the assurance that they were "framing" the landscape artfully, thus making "art" out of nature, and so were eligible for acceptance by their European confrères.[40]

Some landscape painters resorted to classical conventions in the American landscapes they exhibited in Europe. Known as the American Claude[41], Thomas Doughty (1793-1856) painted one of his more idealized American landscapes, *Anthony's Nose, Lake George* (no. 10), during his stay in London in 1837-38. Though probably based on a sketch of the actual site,[42] the view of the famous New York mountain is set within a typical classical format, with a dark foreground, brightly illuminated body of water in the middle distance, and a winding shoreline leading along a series of diagonals into the hazy, sun-struck distance. The subordinate trees at right answer a large, symmetrically branching tree opposite, providing a natural frame for the tranquil river. Where Claude would have posed classical ruins or an arcadian temple in op-

position to the foreground tree, Doughty raised the sun-struck form of the mountain, substituting American nature for European ruins as a source of associations to a pastoral ideal. The generalized rendering of forms relates to Reynolds' promotion of the simplifying approach to painting nature, so as to achieve an ideal of perfect beauty. The emphasis, therefore, is on a blurring of outlines, an overall softness and atmospheric warmth of the stilled forms. A warm brown tonality unifies the composition and contributes to a mood of poetic tranquility that would have appealed to a British audience schooled in the landscapes of Claude and Gaspard.

Claude's golden, light-filled sky was the common denominator of American paintings of the beautiful. Asher Durand (1796-1886) created a poetic reverie of the American landscape in *A Peaceful Day, Sunset* of 1870 (no. 13). Durand founded his career in the 1830s on pastoral scenes of country villages and seasonal labors drenched in Claudian sunlight and rendered in a manner suggestive of the British classical painters. In this painting, Durand merged Claude's conventions with an attention to the spaciousness of American scenery. *A Peaceful Day* presents a vision of domesticated nature that expresses the presence of a benevolent deity in the gentle light. As in the pastoral arcadia of Claude, man appears in complete harmony with nature. The farmer makes his way up the well-worn road to his comfortable house, while a party of landed gentry takes in the spectacle of the setting sun from the shelter of a grove of trees. The interaction of the opposed groups of trees provide an unobtrusive frame for the panoramic vista of pastures and hills receding into the pastel horizon. Turner used a similar frame of trees around a sun-struck expanse of gently receding British landscape in the "Junction of the Severn and the Wye," 1811, from the *Liber Studiorum* (no. 5). This Claudian format is translated into a composition of beautiful American nature in Durand's painting. Durand offers the sun, in the cloud-filled sky and on the reflecting surface of the still lake, as the "divine attribute"[43] of the landscape most profoundly eloquent in speaking of God's presence in nature.

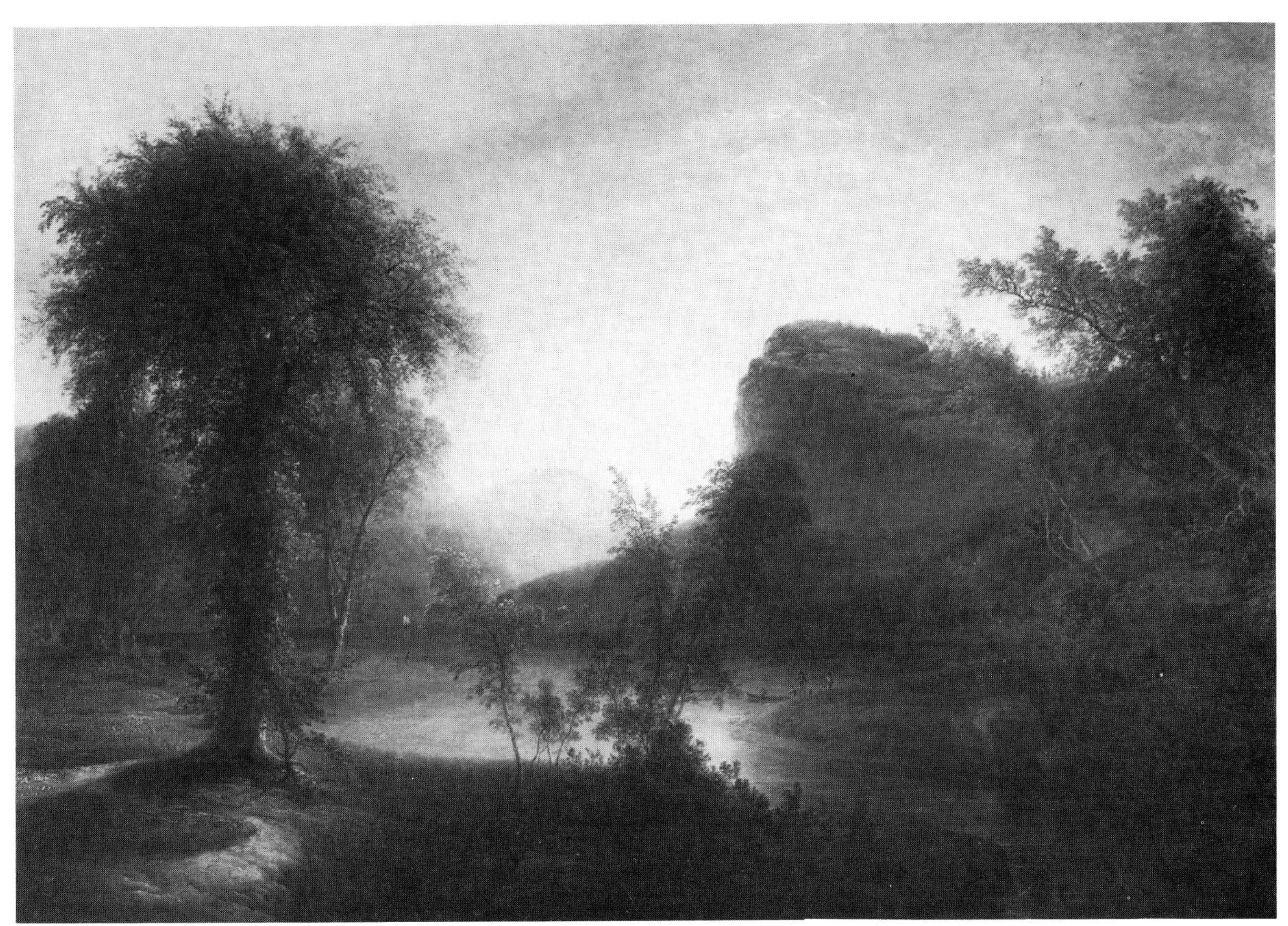

Thomas Doughty. *Anthony's Nose, Lake George, N.Y.*, 1837-38 (no.10)

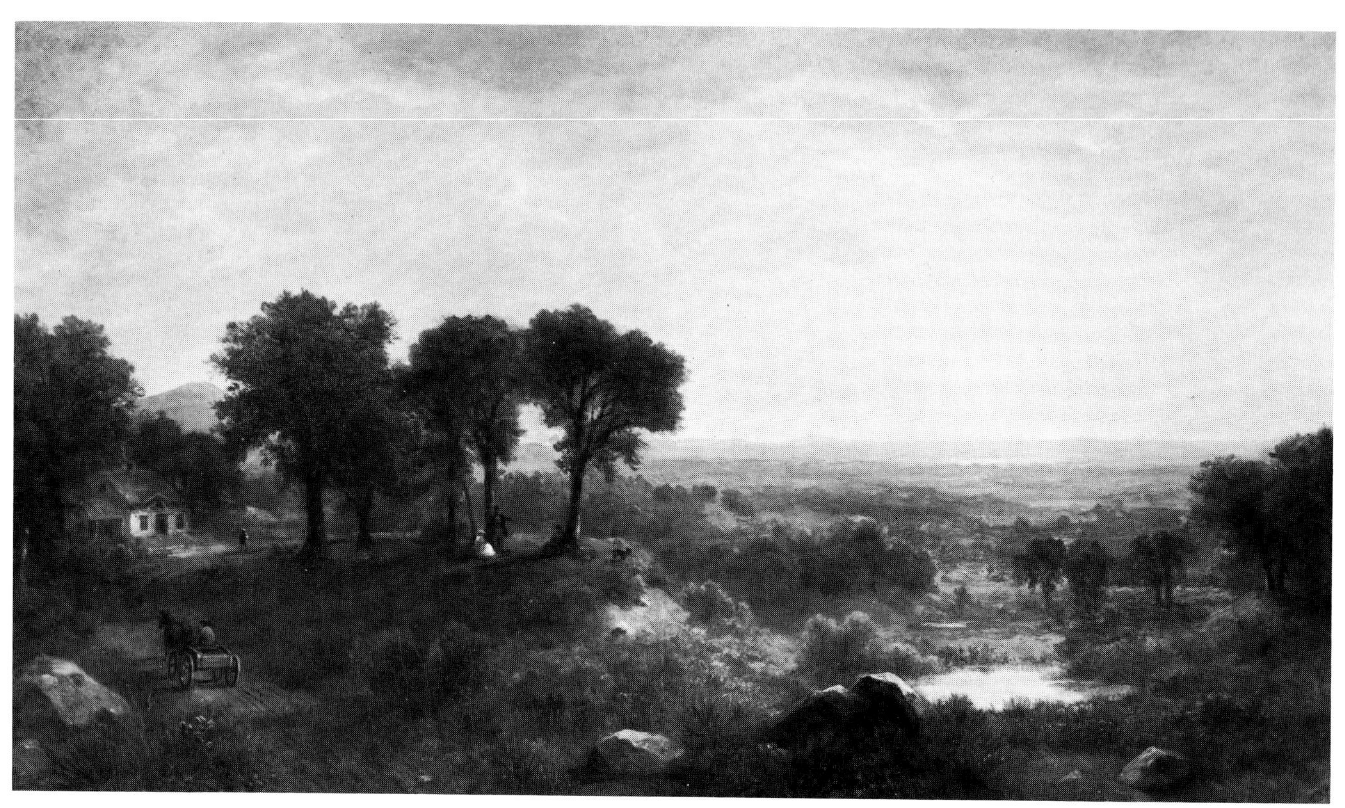

Asher B. Durand. *Landscape, A Peaceful Day, Sunset*, 1870 (no.13)

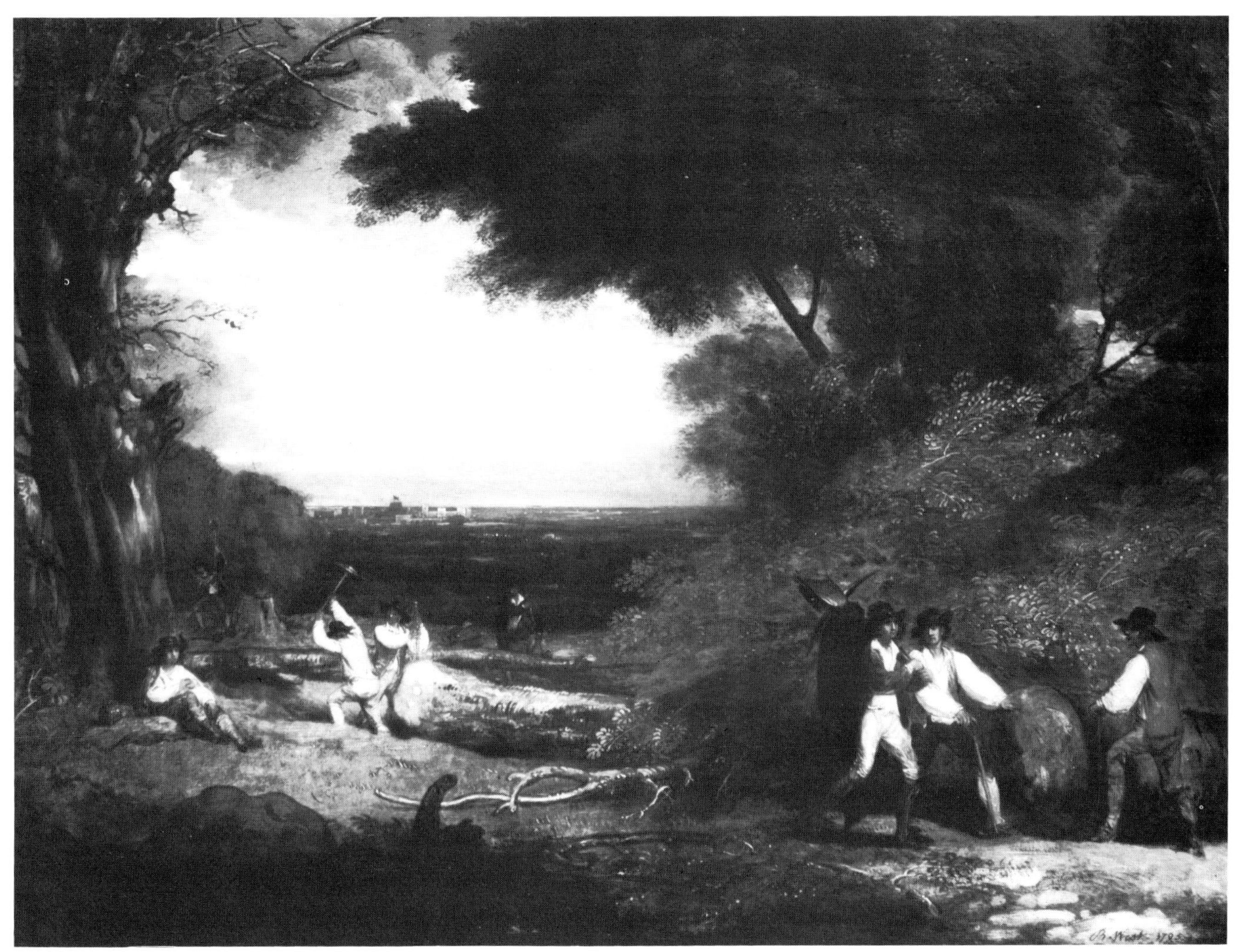

Benjamin West. *Woodcutters in Windsor Park*, 1795 (no.25)

THE PICTURESQUE

While the classical, ideal approach to landscape became a means for American artists to express the inspirational beauty of their native country, the picturesque mode was especially popular with 19th-century American landscape painters as a means of asserting the landscape's visual variety and associational appeal. The principal writers on the picturesque were well-known to American readers within a few years of their British debuts. William Gilpin's "On Picturesque Beauty," from *Three Essays* (1792, no. 19), was reprinted in an American journal in 1793.[44] An 1800 article, "On a Taste for the Picturesque," recommended Gilpin as "one writer...eminent for displaying the principles of landscape...whose works ought to be perfectly familiar to every mind endowed with virtuous propensities and true taste."[45] Americans read Gilpin's *Tours* and other treatises for their suggestions on the creation of balanced compositions from wild scenery. Gilpin showed American artists that an arrangement of landscape elements into a composition could, as Cole said, "surpass in beauty and effect any picture painted from a single view."[46] Gilpin determined specific visual qualities Americans could discover in their own landscape and compositional formulas painters could adapt to native subjects. His enthusiasm for wild scenery as the most picturesque type of landscape helped influence his American readers to consider the picturesqueness of their own wilderness.

In the early American literary circles, writers expressed a romantic interest in their native landscape. The years of relative peace and prosperity following the Revolution saw the publication of numerous travel books devoted to American scenery. William Bartram's *Travels Through North and South Carolina, Georgia, East and West Florida* (1792) and Alexander Wilson's *The Foresters: Description of a Pedestrian Tour of the Fall of Niagara* (1804) are typical examples. Magazines like the *Portfolio* and *Atkinson's Casket* published illustrated essays on American scenery early in the century. The later *New-York Mirror* (1823-42) and *The Knickerbocker* (1833-65) included numerous articles on American landscape and its painters by such distinguished authors as Washington Irving, James Fenimore Cooper, and William Cullen Bryant. These writers, the most familiar of the so-called Knickerbocker group of American authors, preceded the Hudson River School painters in focusing attention on the American landscape. All three writers constantly referred to the "picturesque" qualities of American scenery, and comparisons between the "nature poets" and the landscape painters have revealed many parallel British influences.[47]

The efforts of American picturesque writers and painters were merged in publications like *American Scenery* (1840, no. 49), with essays on well-known American sites by the Knickerbocker writer Nathaniel Parker Willis and engravings after drawings by the English landscape painter William Henry Bartlett (1809-54). *The Home Book of the Picturesque* (1852) brought together the writings of Irving, Cooper, and Bryant with engravings after Cole, Durand, and Church to celebrate American scenery. Though some of the authors discussed the more awesome elements of the landscape, the majority attempted to find American examples of picturesque variety and contrast. Bayard Taylor's singing praise of "the variety of landscape" in Pennsylvania marks out the Juniata River for its "picturesque beauty." Taylor discusses it with a peculiarly American emphasis on repose quite different from the parameters of Gilpin's picturesque:

> Here is nothing grand or awe-inspiring. The outlines of the mountains in the background, though clearly drawn in the serene air, are soft, graceful, and suggestive only of repose; the nearer crags, though bluff and rude, are mantled with foliage, and the quiet curve of the transparent water, touched with the gleam of a pigmy sail in the distance, whispers of other nooks and more beautiful retreats, far away in the silent solitudes of the hills. The freshness of those scenes has not yet departed; the dew of the virgin continent is still moist upon them.[48]

It is evident from the works of American picturesque writers and artists that the picturesque was a multivalent term,

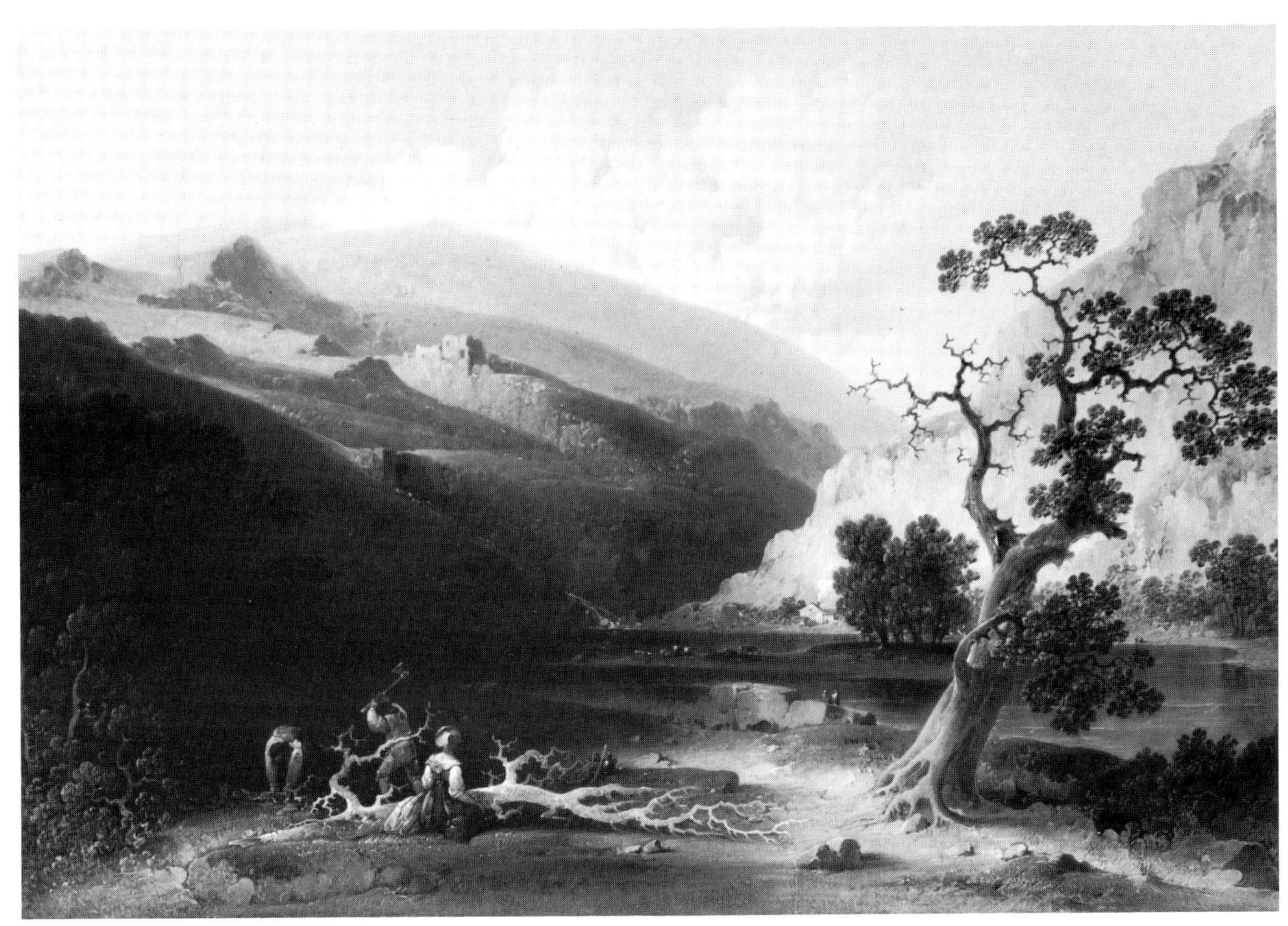

Joshua Shaw. *The Pioneers*, ca. 1838 (no.30)

connoting more of the individual's joy of discovery of a paintable scene than any specific application to the tenets of British theorists. The elements that unified the various 18th-century writers' notions of what was picturesque — Gilpin's "roughness," Price's "sudden variation" — were maintained intact by American artists. "Picturesque" essentially became synonymous with "varied" or "diverse," a quality of interplay and contrast perceived in its purest form in the carpet of colors thrown over a landscape during autumn or a mixture of settled and wild landscape. A picturesque scene could incorporate aspects of nature that previous generations of British connoisseurs would have regarded as beautiful or sublime. One of the peculiar characteristics of the works of American picturesque painters, such as Jasper Cropsey and Thomas Doughty, is the combination of intimacy and vastness contained within a single carefully composed landscape. Where the attention to details of foliage, figures, and flickering light in the foreground recalls Price's stress on the close observation of nature, the often enormous scale of the background clearly responds to the vastness of America.

One of the earliest examples of American painting in the picturesque mode is Benjamin West's 1795 *Woodcutters in Windsor Park* (no. 25). His largest and most ambitious work in this genre, it depicts the reshaping of the royal grounds to provide an unobstructed view of the Queen's hunting lodge.[49] Its contrast of a darkly shadowed foreground to a broadly light-struck background reflects contemporary British conventions of the picturesque. The use of framing trees, the broad contrasts of shadow and sunlight, and the sketchy quality of the rugged foreground foliage and debris recall the format of William Gilpin's picturesque drawings, such as the *Landscape with River Valley* (no. 17). Contrary to Gilpin, though, and closer to the advice of Uvedale Price and later writers, West adds a number of stalwart laborers to this scene, creating a genre incident that hearkens back to the integration of native landscape and English rustic types in the work of Thomas Gainsborough. In this typically English landscape, West appears as the first of a long line of American artists to reflect the influence of British painting and aesthetics.

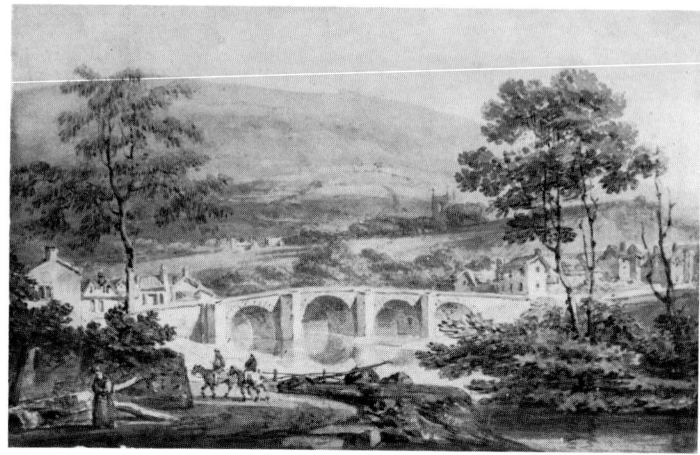

Joseph M.W. Turner. *Matlock*, 1794 (no.20)

The calm and serenity Bayard Taylor noted in his description of Pennsylvania provide the mood for a very early American landscape by the immigrant English painter Joshua Shaw (ca. 1777-1860). Shaw was one of the more talented and successful of the second wave of European landscape painters. *Landscape with Cattle* (no. 26) is dated 1818, the year after Shaw settled in Philadelphia. The gently rolling mountains and clusters of farm buildings suggest rural Pennsylvania. In composition and motifs, Shaw's painting evokes comparison with a 1794 watercolor of the town of Matlock on the river Derwent (no. 20) by his contemporary, Turner. In this small watercolor Turner created a lively view of the town hugging the edge of a broad mountain. Shaw amplified the scope of his scene and offered in the right background an immense view dissolving into the luminous horizon. His landscape compares to Turner's in its partition of the scene into three spatial zones, the still river reflecting an arched bridge, the buildings on the banks, and the tower-like structure on the mountainside. The Claudian framing trees, silhouetted against the blue mountain in Turner's watercolor, are replaced by vibrant masses of crisply delineated foliage. The

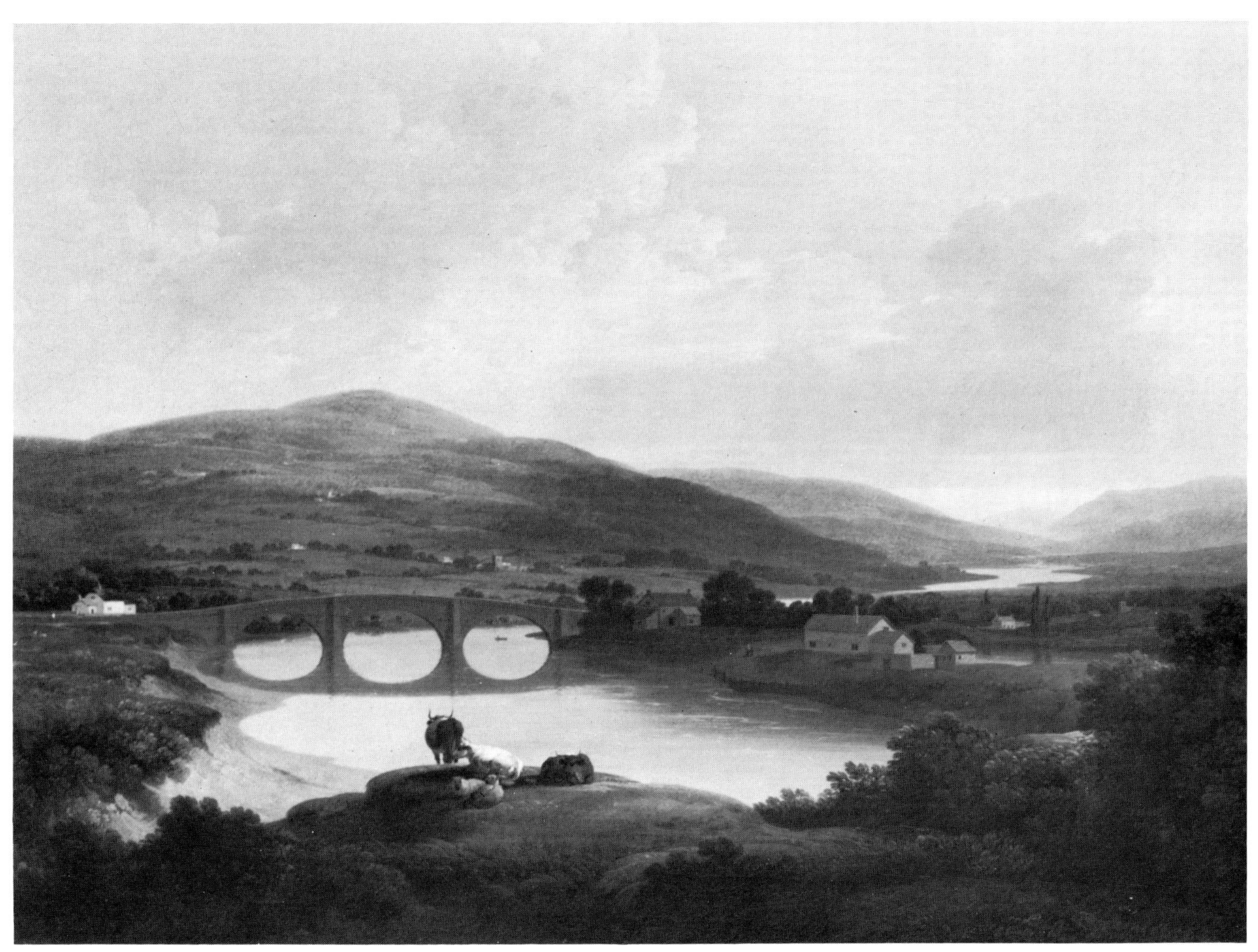

Joshua Shaw. *Landscape with Cattle*, 1818 (no.26)

grazing cows and sheep on the platform-like clearing are emblematic of the benevolence of this landscape.

In his later landscapes, Shaw continued to create picturesque compositions, revealing how closely this immigrant artist followed the earlier styles of British landscape painting. *The Pioneers,* ca. 1838 (no. 30), places an imaginary foreground before a landscape suggesting the scale and choppy profile of the Delaware Water Gap. While the imposing mountains are sublime, the ragged outlines of the leaning, gesticulating tree and the seething vitality of the foliage and figures establish the picturesque character of the scene. Frontiersmen hewing a fallen trunk and the enframing tree at right recall similar motifs in paintings by Gainsborough and West (nos. 14 & 25). In spite of the sweeping background, the composition seems intimate and contained. An especially interesting element is a geological outcropping of the mountainside that resembles a ruined castle. Wishing to make his landscape American but conforming to the suggestions of the English theorists, Shaw fashioned a mysterious relic, an American equivalent of the picturesque ruin.

Among the first generation of Hudson River School artists, Thomas Cole (1801-48) was interested in the picturesque from an early date in his career. References to the variety and contrast of American scenery as its greatest attraction fill his writings. Cole often embarked on what he termed ''tours of the picturesque''[50] during the summers and falls after he settled in Catskill, New York, in 1836. In his journal he noted the serene beauty of an October day in the Catskills:

> The day was such a one as we should have chosen, one of our heavenly autumnal days, when the sun shines blandly through a clear and cloudless sky, and the crystal atmosphere casts a veil of beauty over the landscape, rich with the loveliest tints.[51]

This mix of serenity and variety characterizing autumn in the American forest is also apparent in Cole's *Sunset in the Cats-kills* (no. 31). Seen as if in a proscenium, an intimate tableau of stilled nature unfolds beneath a sky saturated with the golden light of the setting sun. A broad lake spreads across the middle-ground, bearing a solitary boatman, who, back turned to us, observes the pageant of autumn. Gilpin's dark foreground is replaced by the lake pouring into the viewer's space. Our eyes are drawn immediately to the shimmering surface of the waters and then back to the halo of forest and purple mountains. Irregular and writhing tree forms are distributed along the bank, where Cole has indulged his powers of observation of natural effects. This realism contrasts to the deliberate artifice of the enframing arch and its echo in the leaning trees.

Autumn was, in Price's estimation, ''the painter's season,''[52] when the colors of nature are of the proper variety, depth, and richness to make them inspirations for a picture. The season especially conveys associations to the brevity of life. British artists and poets, however, rarely painted their own landscape in fall colors, perhaps due to the lack of any striking effects.[53] In his ''Essay on American Scenery'' (1836) Thomas Cole echoed British aesthetics in his statements on the picturesqueness of fall:

> There is one season when the American forest surpasses all the world in gorgeousness; — then every hill and dale is riant in the luxury of color — every hue is there, from the liveliest green to deepest purple — from the most golden yellow to the intensest crimson. The artist looks despairingly upon the glowing landscape, and in the old world his truest imitations of the American forest, at this season, are called falsely bright, and scenes in Fairy Land.[54]

Jasper F. Cropsey (1823-1900) became the pre-eminent painter of the American autumn, and in massive canvases like *Autumn on the Hudson River,* 1860 (National Gallery of Art), he actually elicited the response Cole described from the amazed British.[55] During the 1850s, Cropsey experimented with new pigments to create the effects of autumn foliage. *The Hudson at Piermont* of 1852 (no. 35) puts far into the background the title subject, reducing the presence of the Hudson to a small sun-struck wedge containing the thin spit of land connected by railroad to the town of Piermont. The pic-

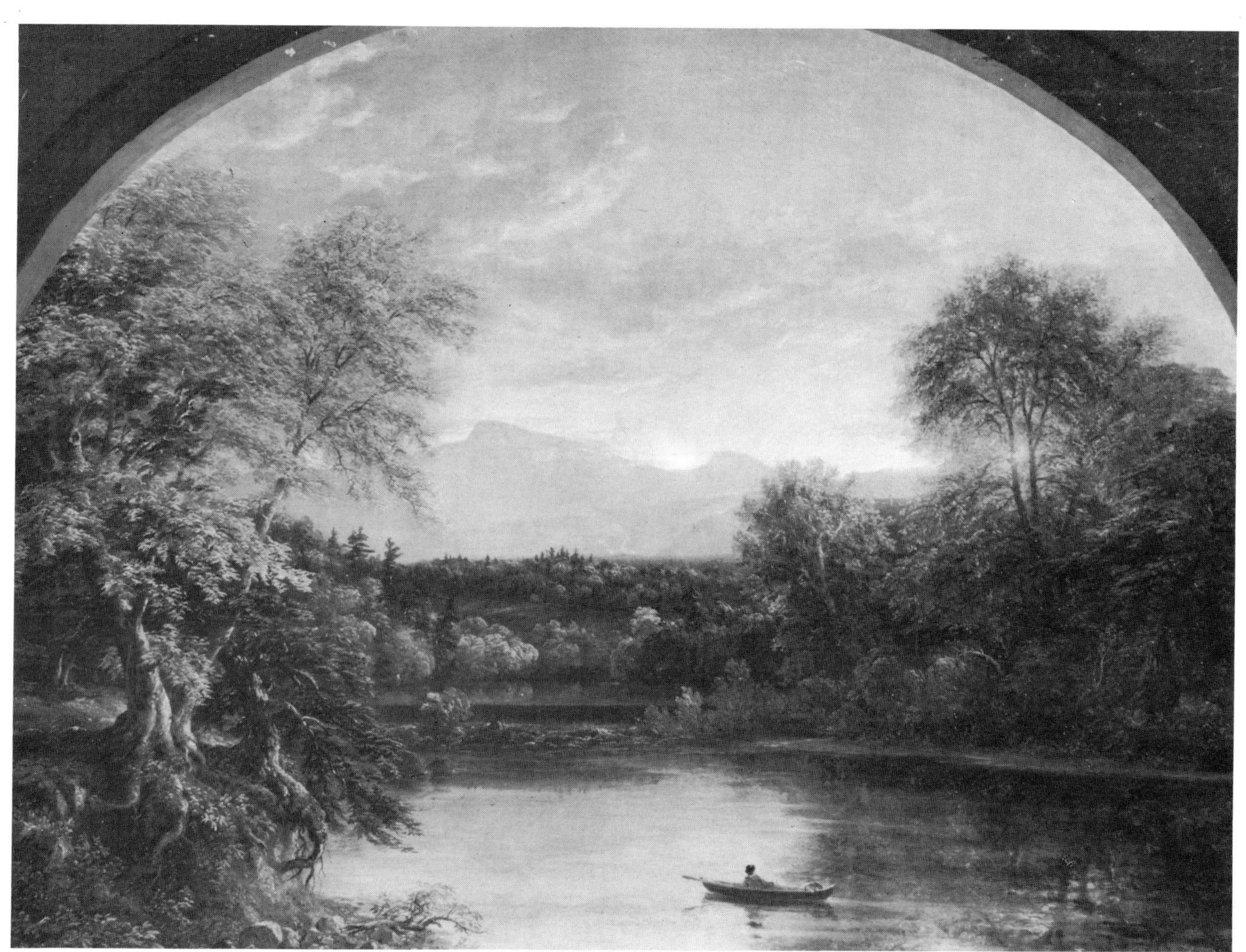

Thomas Cole. *Sunset in the Catskills*, 1841 (no.31)

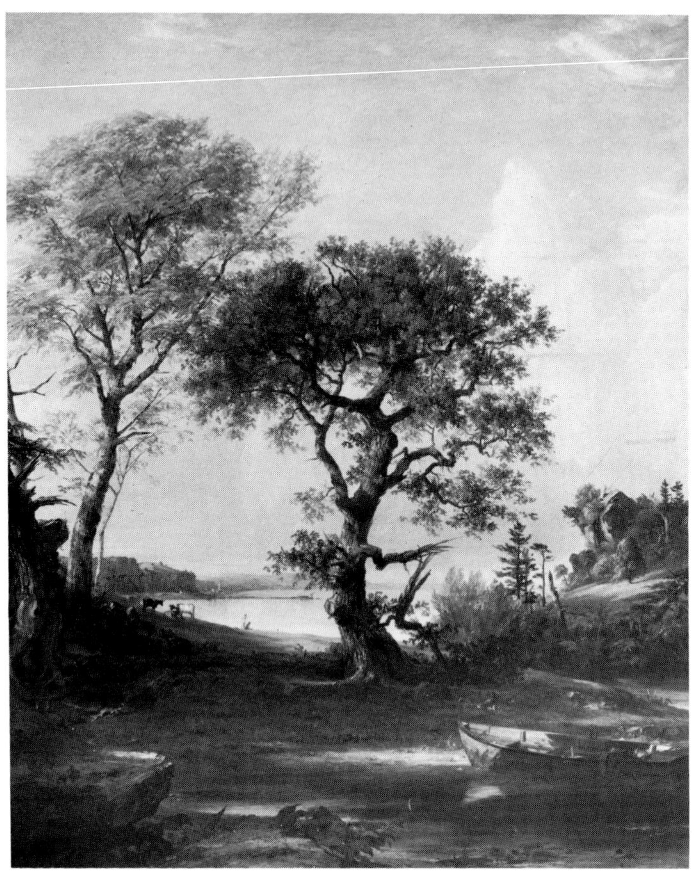

Jasper F. Cropsey.
The Hudson at Piermont, 1852 (no.35)

used moist, thick pigments to render the rough bark of the tree trunks. Cropsey's sensitivity to the aesthetic differences among trees compares to the ruminations of William Gilpin and Uvedale Price. His inspired record of light filtering through sprays of branches and pooling up amid the shadows of the foreground relates Cropsey's manner to the realism of Asher Durand.

Asher Durand (1796-1886) was the foremost proponent of a morally-inspired realism in the depiction of American landscape. He was one of the most successful engravers in the country when, in 1825, he first encountered the early Catskill landscapes of Thomas Cole. Durand and Cole became close friends, and Cole's example led Durand to take up landscape painting in the 1830s.[56] After an early period of pastoral landscapes and allegories in the classical tradition, Durand developed a type of plein-air oil sketching unprecedented in American painting for its attention to the objective appearance of nature. ''Truth to nature'' was Durand's standard, but only insofar as the artist could express the spirit animating nature:

> The external appearance of this our dwelling-place, apart from its wondrous structure and functions that minister to our well-being, is fraught with lessons of high and holy meaning, only surpassed by the light of the Revelation.[57]

The *Woodland Landscape* (no. 34) is a picturesque composition Durand favored. This design divided the scene into a dark, detailed foreground, a lighter middleground with a grove of trees or a forested hillside, and a view off one side into the misty distance. Typically, Durand chose an isolated fragment of nature, the edge of a forest and a shallow pool, and employed a variety of brushwork and colors to suggest the intricate diversity of form and texture in the wilderness. Observing his subject closely, he brings the birches forward to the viewer. Such fresh intimacy and human scale gives the viewer the sensation of being inside the sun-dappled woodland, and links Durand to the objectives of Price and the later picturesque writers and artists in Britain.

turesque contrasts to be found in nature form the actual subject, as seen in the two foreground trees, one a strong, young specimen of lighter hue and the other a darker, weatherbeaten tree with hacked and broken branches. The serpentine line of the curving shore recalls Gainsborough in such compositions as the early *View in Suffolk* (no. 14); both artists

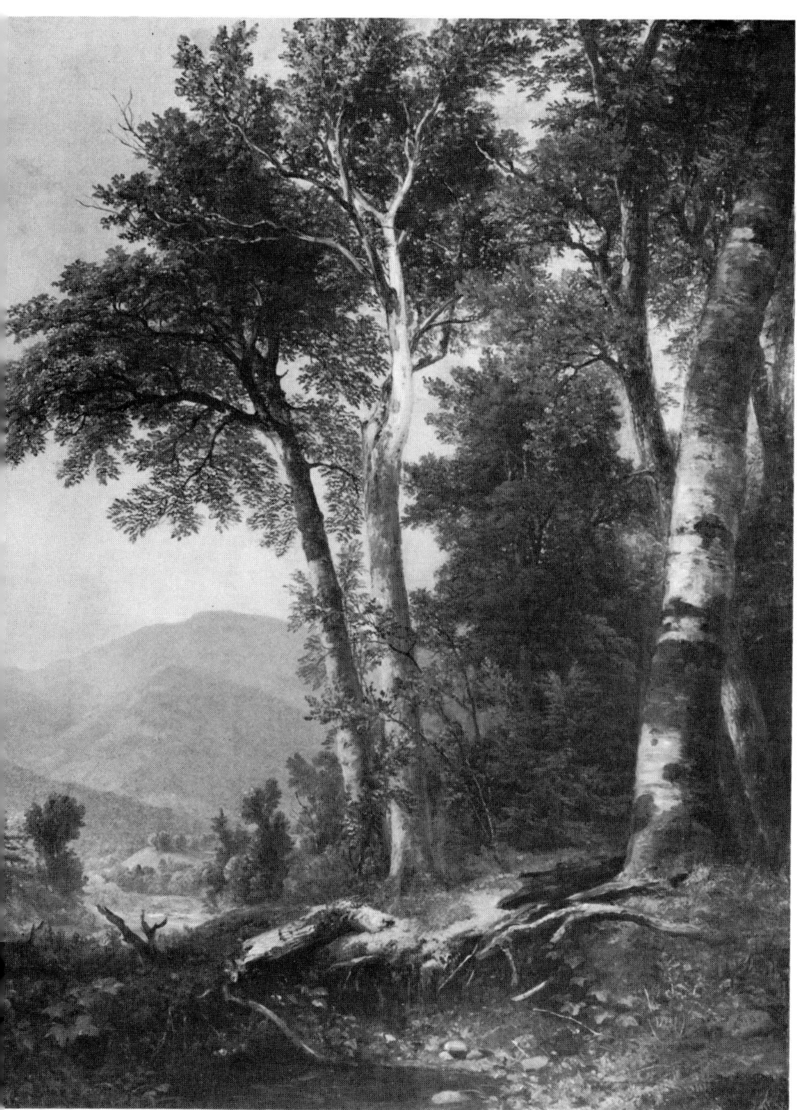

Asher B. Durand. *Woodland Landscape* (no.34)

THE SUBLIME

The primitive wilderness inspired a third mode in American landscape painting, the sublime. References to the awe and reverence induced by the sublime grandeur and immensity of American nature fill early travel literature. Thaddeus Mason Harris, in his *Journal of a Tour into the Territory Northwest of the Allegheny Mountains* (1805), wrote that "the majestic features of the uncultivated wilderness" expand the imagination and "rouse an admiration exalting as it is delightful...THE SUBLIME IN NATURE, which, in its effect is equally solemn and pleasing, captivates while it awes, and charms while it elevates and expands the soul."[58] Such statements reveal how early in American culture Burke's theory was known and accepted as an authoritative aesthetic for articulating a response to the American landscape. The untamed, savage, and turbulent elements of the wilderness served as some of the earliest subjects for American landscape painters.

Of all the early American landscape painters, Cole was most responsive to the sublime in his native scenery. Vast areas of wilderness distinguished American from European scenery; and in the great mountains and forests of New York and New England, Cole discovered "the consequent associations are of God the creator — they are his undefiled works."[59] Cole's striking contrasts of luminous and stormy skies, his broken mountain terrains filled with storm-blasted trees and sun-struck boulders pictorially render the sublime. Some of Cole's most spectacular American landscapes of the 1820s and 30s fruitfully compare to the awesome mountain scenes of Turner.

The excited response of American landscape painters to European mountain scenery may owe a measure of influence to Turner's paintings of these subjects. Thomas Cole missed Switzerland on his first European tour, but on his second, in 1841, he was stupefied by the illimitable grandeur of the Alps, for which he could find no American equivalent. On his return to America, he painted *In the Simmental* (no. 51), which evokes the fantastic mountain masses of Switzerland against a rolling, cloud-filled sky. There was little precedent

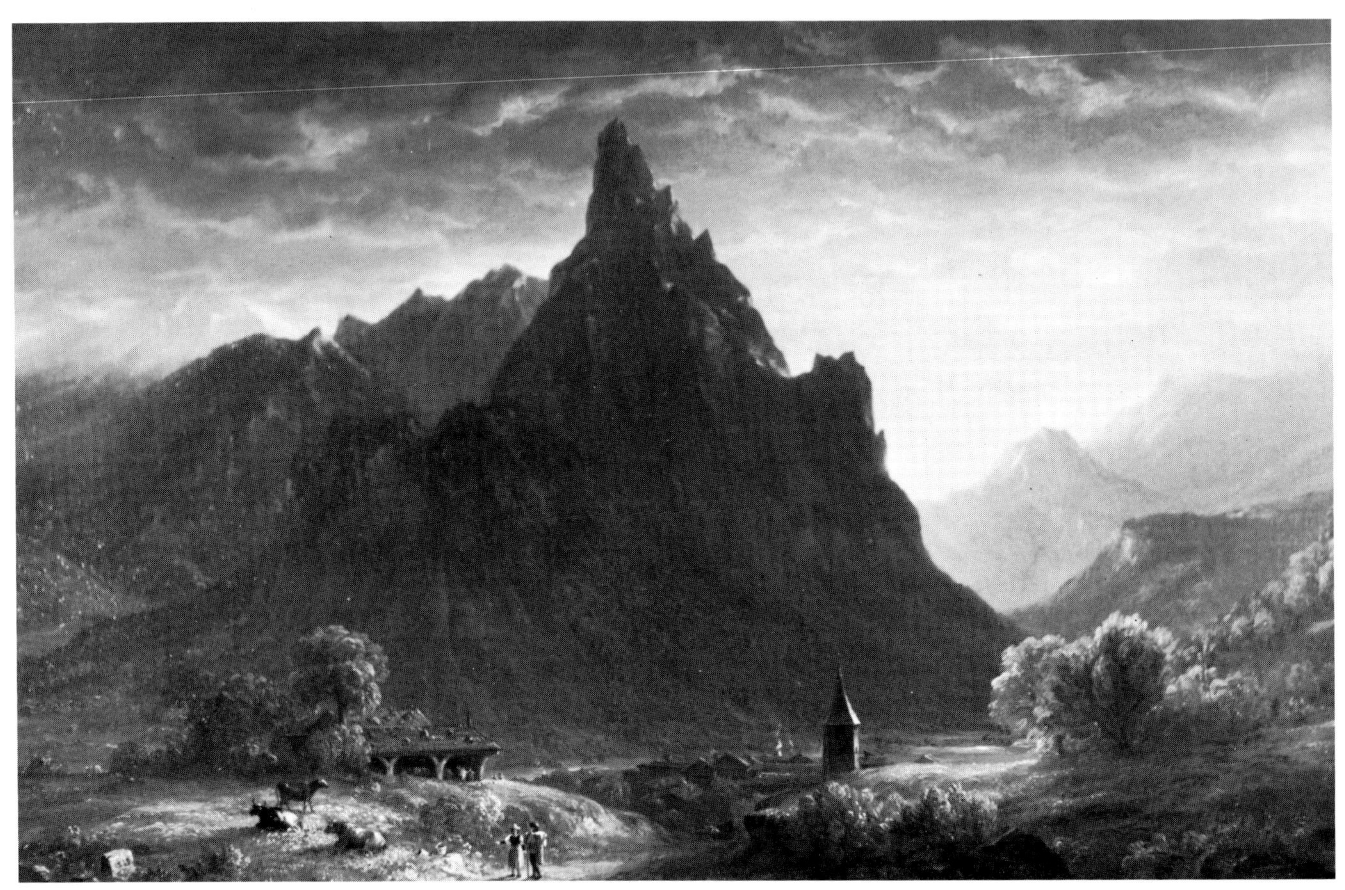

Thomas Cole. *In the Simmental, Switzerland*, 1843 (no.51)

in American art for Alpine subjects. Though it is not documented, Cole seems to have referred to the British school of mountain painting (nos. 36 and 38) for the powerful mountain silhouette and churning atmosphere. Cole's scene tempers the awesomeness of this environment by including tiny buildings, meadows, and figures in a manner that recalls Turner's *Picturesque Views of England and Wales* (1838, no. 44). In the end, the vast scale, dramatic atmosphere, and barren forms of this painting outweigh the picturesque motifs of the foreground and convey a response to the terrific sublime.

The work of several later American painters maintained the identification of the sublime with awe-inspiring nature. For the most part, though, displays of a hostile terrain or raging elements were not in keeping with the American concept of a benevolent God in nature. As early as 1833, when Cole exhibited a ferocious *Tornado* at the National Academy, a writer for *The Knickerbocker* assailed Burke's theory for its foundation in terror and referred to a conception of the sublime that predated Burke. This sublime was an experience of divinity brought on by "an impression or idea of infinitude,"[60] and the sensation provoked was not one of fear, but of a kind of transcendent bliss.

The American insistence on the presentation of God's power and majesty in nature profoundly altered the traditional terrific sublime. William L. Sonntag's 1854 *Mountain Landscape* (no. 53) reflects the influence of Cole's wilderness scenes in its dramatic depiction of a mist-shrouded mountain hulk guarded in the foreground by a dense legion of spiky trees. The dramatic diagonals and awesome wilderness in Sonntag's painting are also striking in comparison to Turner's *Chamonix* (no. 38). Unlike Turner's painting, this one offers no visible sign of man's presence. The viewer confronts the virgin wilderness, and the immense mountain looming over the scene is an emblem of a powerful God, Durand's "Great Designer."[61] As J. Gray Sweeney has pointed out, the three storm-blasted trees at the left edge of the scene have obvious Christian connotations.[62] The generally forbidding character of the foreground suggests the difficulties of this imperfect world, the travails of the spirit in its journey to the Godhead.

The range of trees clinging to the hillsides, some in full foliage and others denuded and skeletal, presents the drama of life and death in the American forest. Such sublime elements reveal God in nature: "...the mountains and the oceans, the forest and the river...are manifestations of the moral and inner life of the world, of the Eternal Mind whose thoughts are constant laws" (*North American Review*, 1855).[63]

Frederic E. Church's (1826-1900) 1865 portrayal of *Mount Desert Island* (no. 59) continues the subject matter and scale of the traditional sublime. Unlike Sonntag, Church provides a clearing for the viewer, who, from a vantage point high above the ocean, is witness to the sublime spectacle of clouds breaking up after a storm. The only human reference is the spot-like presence of a sailboat on the dark waters. The landscape is locked into breathless silence; a deer, issuing forth from the shadowy forest at right, is a fugitive element of wildlife in an otherwise motionless, primeval land. The clouds at left rush into the scene like divine messengers in a Baroque ceiling. This operatic celebration of American nature reflects Turner's sublime landscape style. The broadly elliptical design, binding land and sky in a dynamic union of form and atmosphere, compares directly with the similar configuration in Turner's "Ben Arthur" from the *Liber Studiorum* (no. 40). Church was the one American artist most frequently compared to Turner, and the heightened color and turbulent action of the sky in *Mount Desert Island* suggest the British painter's influence. Coming at the close of the Civil War, this painting expresses through American nature the hopes of a nation for rebirth and harmony.

Church's influence on later American landscape painting is seen in the competition to create ever-larger and more impressive paintings of sublime scenery. Albert Bierstadt (1830-1902) and Thomas Hill (1829-1908) succeeded Church with their colossal renditions of the natural wonders of the Rocky Mountains, Yosemite, and the Pacific Northwest (nos. 57-58). Their art reflects the American concept of Manifest Destiny, a cultural imperative that led to the linking of the coasts by railroad and travel to remote regions of North and South America in search of the sublime. The spiritual en-

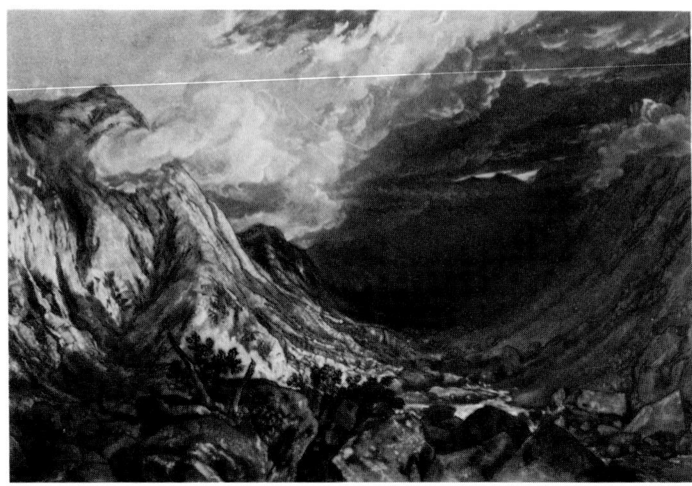

Thomas Lupton after Joseph M.W. Turner.
"Ben Arthur, Scotland," 1819, *Liber Studiorum* (no.40)

thusiasm with which Cole and Durand wrote of and painted the eastern wilderness found new expression in canvases that unite a feeling for huge open spaces and a naturalist's dedication to accurate detail. Such paintings carried the excitement of the traditional sublime to the end of the 19th century, as painters attempted to match in scale and pictorial theatrics the awesome natural wonders encountered in the settling of the West.

In contrast to the heroic sublime of Church and the western painters, certain mid-century artists, now referred to as "luminists," offered a "transcendental sublime" that depended more on order, stillness, and harmonic color than on the grand scale and dynamism of the older sublime.[64] Certain principles of the landscape — space, light, atmosphere — replaced nature's awe-inspiring forms as the subjects of the luminist painters. Contemporary American literature mirrored this shift to a more tranquil, contemplative mood in American landscape. The Transcendentalist authors, Ralph Waldo Emerson, Henry David Thoreau, and Margaret

Fuller, experienced nature as the embodiment of spiritual truths. Emerson's famous lines from his 1836 essay "Nature" have often been invoked to suggest the luminist painter's spiritual immersion in nature:

> In the woods is perpetual youth. Within these plantations of God, a decorum and sanctity reign...In the woods, we return to reason and faith. There I feel that nothing can befall me in life — no disgrace, no calamity (leaving me my eyes), which nature cannot repair. Standing on the bare ground — my head bathed by the blithe air and up-lifted into infinite space — all mean egotism vanishes. I become a transparent eyeball, I am nothing; I see all; the currents of the Universal Being circulate through me; I am part or parcel of God...In the tranquil landscape, and especially in the distant line of the horizon, man beholds somewhat as beautiful as his own nature.[65]

John F. Kensett (1816-72) exhibits the parameters of the luminist sublime in his view of the *Upper Mississippi* of 1854 (no. 54). The traditionally sublime mountains are disposed between the open, light-filled sky and river in quiet harmony. The viewer's space is that of the still, silver river, where alighted ducks and the distant boatmen inhabit the same domain as the cliff's reflections. As in other luminist paintings, light is the unifying element, pictorially and symbolically. In contrast to Burke's preference for "sad and fuscous colors, as black, brown, or deep purple,"[66] luminist painters usually chose lighter colors, delicately modulated within a limited range of hues. In Martin J. Heade's (1819-1904) *Jersey Meadows* (no. 61), the zigzag line of a marsh stream leads the eye into the luminous middle distance. The pervasive light, flooding a massive haystack, and space, extended over the flat plane of the marshes to the tremulous horizon, are the sublime elements of this soundless landscape.

Two 1860s paintings by Sanford Gifford (1823-80) demonstrate the varying responses of a mid-century landscape painter to the sublime in American nature. In portraying a *Storm in the Catskills* (no. 56), he pitted the rolling surge of rain

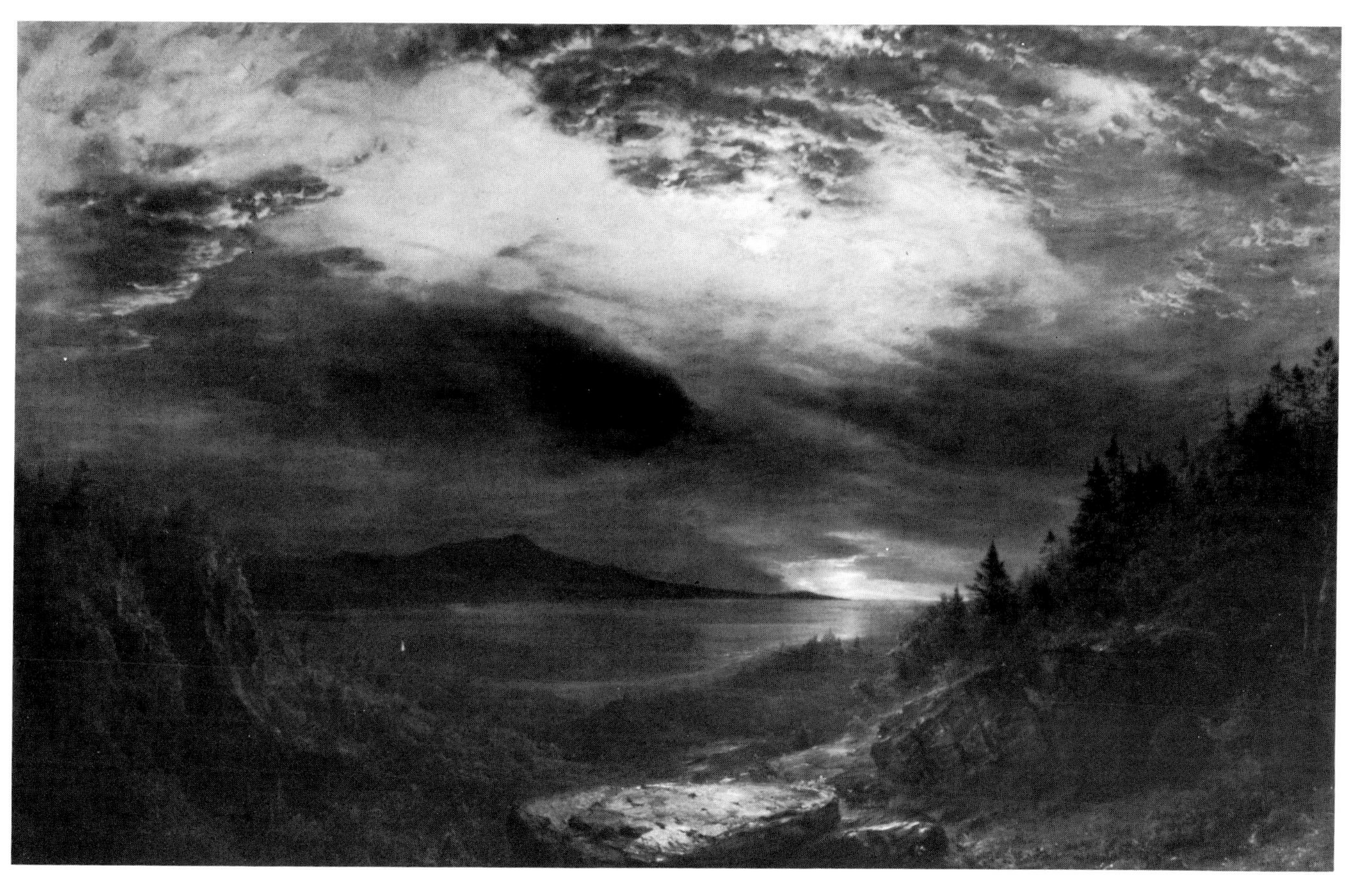

Frederic E. Church. *Mount Desert Island, Maine*, 1865 (no.59)

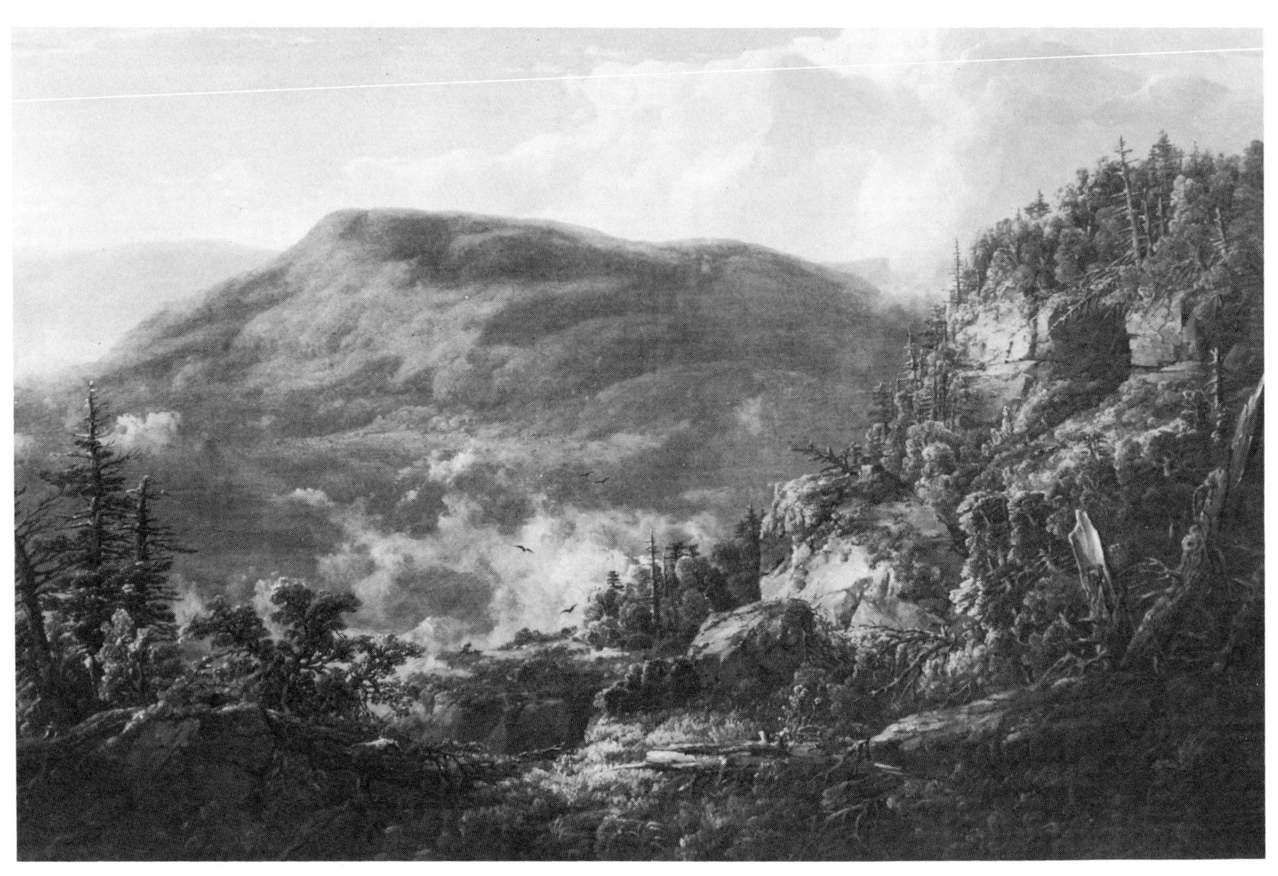

William L. Sonntag. *Mountain Landscape*, 1854 (no.53)

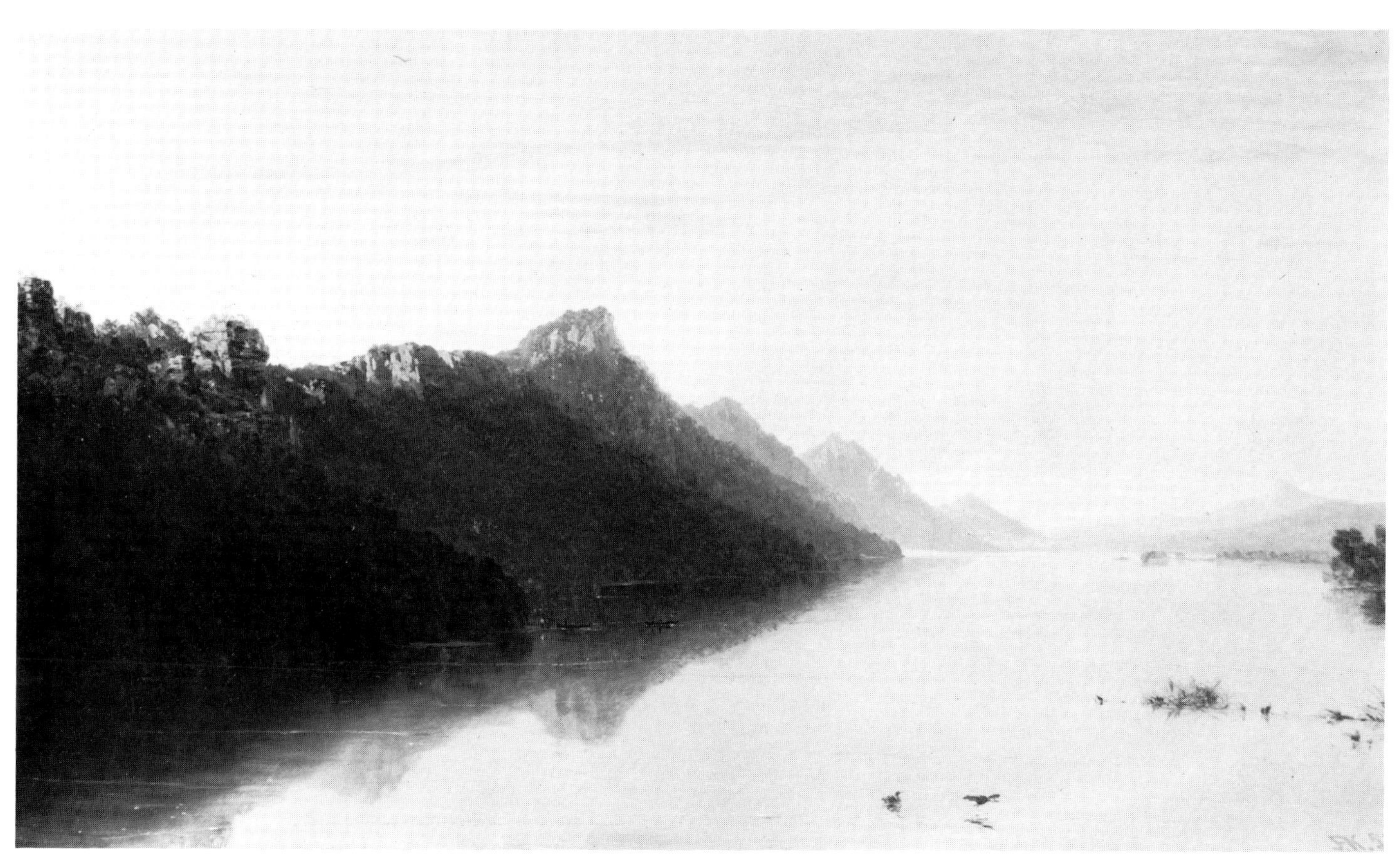

John F. Kensett. *Upper Mississippi*, 1855 (no.54)

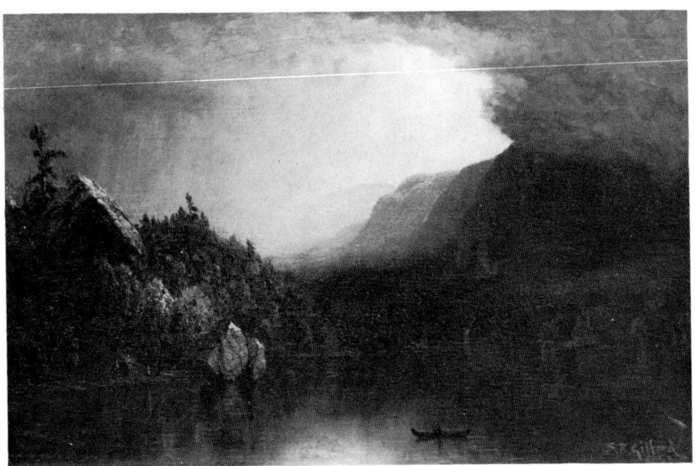

Sanford R. Gifford. *Storm in the Catskills*, 1863 (no.56)

clouds against a rugged mountain landscape. A lone boat-man makes his way to shore in a shroud of darkness. The mood is one of dreadful anticipation, as the elements gather for a violent storm. *Early October in the White Mountains* (no. 55) conveys an entirely different mood. Beneath a cloudless blue sky, cows graze near the edge of a still lake that reflects the trees and range of snow-capped mountains. Gifford renders objects in the foreground with extreme clarity, yet this attention to nature's minutiae does not hinder the sensation of vastness suggested by the panoramic sweep of the background. The peaceful beauty of the White Mountains, rather than the rugged picturesqueness or sublime majesty of the wilderness, is evoked through the serene horizontal emphasis, the still atmosphere, and the subtle tonal gradations. Such luminist canvases suggest an earlier British concept of beauty, rooted in the recognition that "what is beautiful is harmonious and proportionable" and that beauty is perceived by the intellect as "Nature's genuine Order," the ideal harmony existing before original sin.[67]

As a consummate painting of Hudson River School aesthetics, Frederic E. Church's *Sierra Nevada de Santa Mar-*

ta, 1883 (no. 62), metaphorically synthesizes many early American reactions to man, nature, and God. The caravan in this painting embarks on a journey through the dense South American jungle past the immense rise of the Andes. Their explorations lead them through exotic foliage to majestic mountains that dissolve in the rich glow of the sun. Three huge palm trees rising up at one edge, suggestive of crosses in the wilderness, enframe the panoramic expanse of the Andes. Church's interest in the natural sciences, as with others of his generation, fueled his meticulous rendition of geographical and botanical details. But, as he related to the collector Charles Parsons, he "aimed mainly for luminosity":[68] the brilliant light into which all the forms are absorbed is positioned in the visual center of the painting and carries obvious pantheistic overtones. Revolving around the smooth mirror of the lake, this landscape reflects the serene light of classical landscape painting, the grandeur of mountains, and a romantic passion for natural scenery: *The Beautiful, The Sublime, and The Picturesque.* In this, one of his last great paintings, Church created an ambitious statement uniting his artistic ideas at a time when French influences were changing American tastes.

CHURCH noted to Parsons, who commissioned *Sierra Nevada de Santa Marta,* "I hope that you have not been much impressed by the 'Impressionists'. That sort of art is really but one phase of Decorative Art and so easily acquired...It is really very superficial."[69] Against Church's wishes, however, the French Barbizon and Impressionists' influence would come to dominate American painting in the next decade. By the time Church painted *Sierra Nevada de Santa Marta* in 1883 the sublime and beautiful had become antiquated styles for academic showpieces that secured exposition gold medals, but few buyers. Church, Bierstadt, and other masters of the heroic sublime continued to receive honors, but the taste of Americans had begun to shift towards French landscape painting. The picturesque, as well, had seen its heyday in the third quarter of the century, when Cropsey, Durand, and other

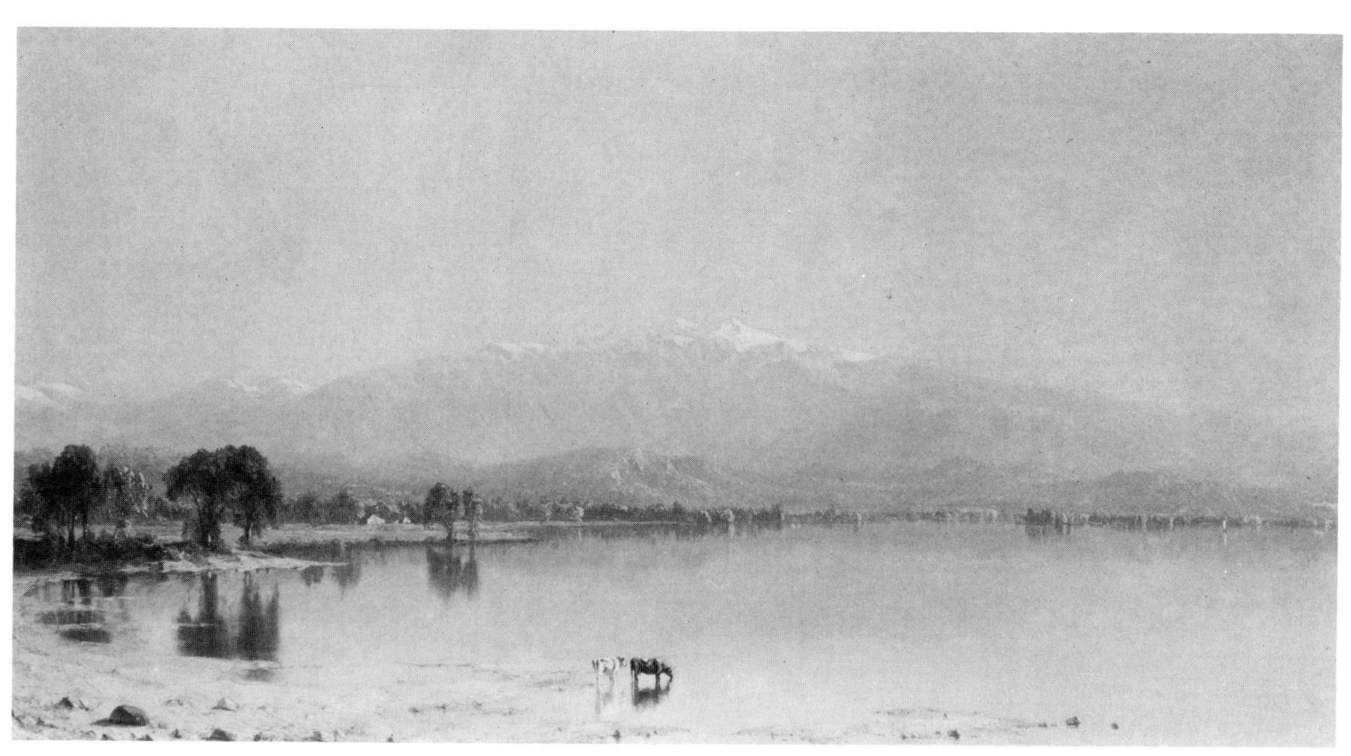

Sanford R. Gifford. *Early October in the White Mountains*, 1860 (no.55)

artists asserted the benevolent associations of settled American nature. With the demographic shift from a rural to an urban population, the picturesque devolved into a format for idealized calendar images of rural arcadia that existed more in the imagination than in reality.

With the achievements of the luminist and epic landscape painters, the long record of America's dialogue with British traditions in landscape art came to a close. Arbiters of American taste gradually regarded the Hudson River School landscapes as archaic and confining. By 1900 the landmark achievements of the 18th-century British and early 19th-century American nature painters were largely ignored. With the rise in the last few decades of scholarship devoted to the painting of this period, we are now, however, in a better position to evaluate the impact of British theory and art on the development of American landscape painting.

The first American landscape painters were British-born and brought to an unpainted continent a background in the contemporary aesthetics of their art. Among these immigrants was Thomas Cole, who had read of the wonders of America as a boy in his native Lancashire. Cole proclaimed in his paintings the power of the American wilderness, and a host of native-born painters — Durand, Kensett, Gifford, Church — heeded his call to render the New World's aesthetic and spiritual riches. Two generations of the Hudson River School freely borrowed from British conventions and aesthetic ideas in developing the first tradition of American landscape painting. The nascent American art academies appropriated the didactic philosophy of Reynolds, with its respect for the classical landscape painters of the 17th century. Americans rendered the Italian landscape in the Claudian format popularized by Wilson and other British painters looking to the past for inspiration. Turning to their own landscape, American painters found confirmation of the aesthetic ideas of the picturesque and the sublime in rural and wild scenery of the vast, virgin continent. The picturesque became a democratic means to appreciate the variety and richness of American scenery. Based in the romantic idea of terror as a stimulus for aesthetic delight, Edmund Burke's conception of the sublime was radically altered by Americans who recognized signs of the deity in the wilds of America. The formulas for the representation of the sublime developed by Cozens, Turner, and other British artists reappeared in the mountain and forest scenes of Cole, Church, and the western painters. An American emphasis on transfiguring light and the harmony of silence, stillness, and compositional order translated the raw sublimity of American landscape into a transcendental poetry of matter and spirit.

In all these imitations, borrowings, and transformations, American artists maintained a fine line between an adherence to European traditions and the forging of original solutions to the problem of creating a national identity. The various aesthetic theories of British art gave them insights into understanding the feelings they had in discovering and depicting a huge, mysterious New World. British painters provided models for them to follow in rendering the limitless variety and power of this wilderness garden. In the process, American artists invested their landscape with associations of a bright future and a progressive present, seeing signs of an eternal pact between God and American civilization in the wonders of their native land.

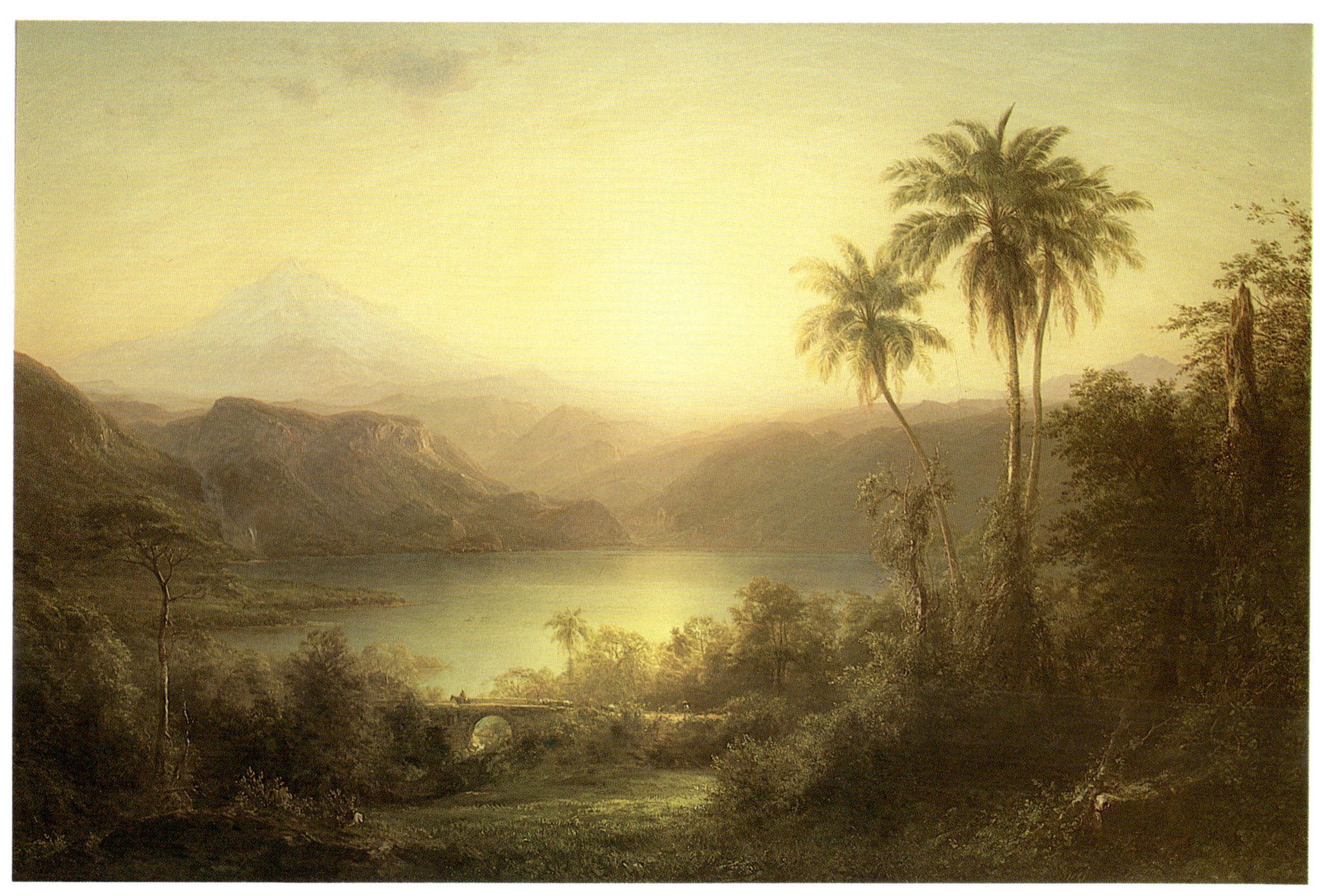

Frederic E. Church. *Sierra Nevada de Santa Marta*, 1883 (no.62)

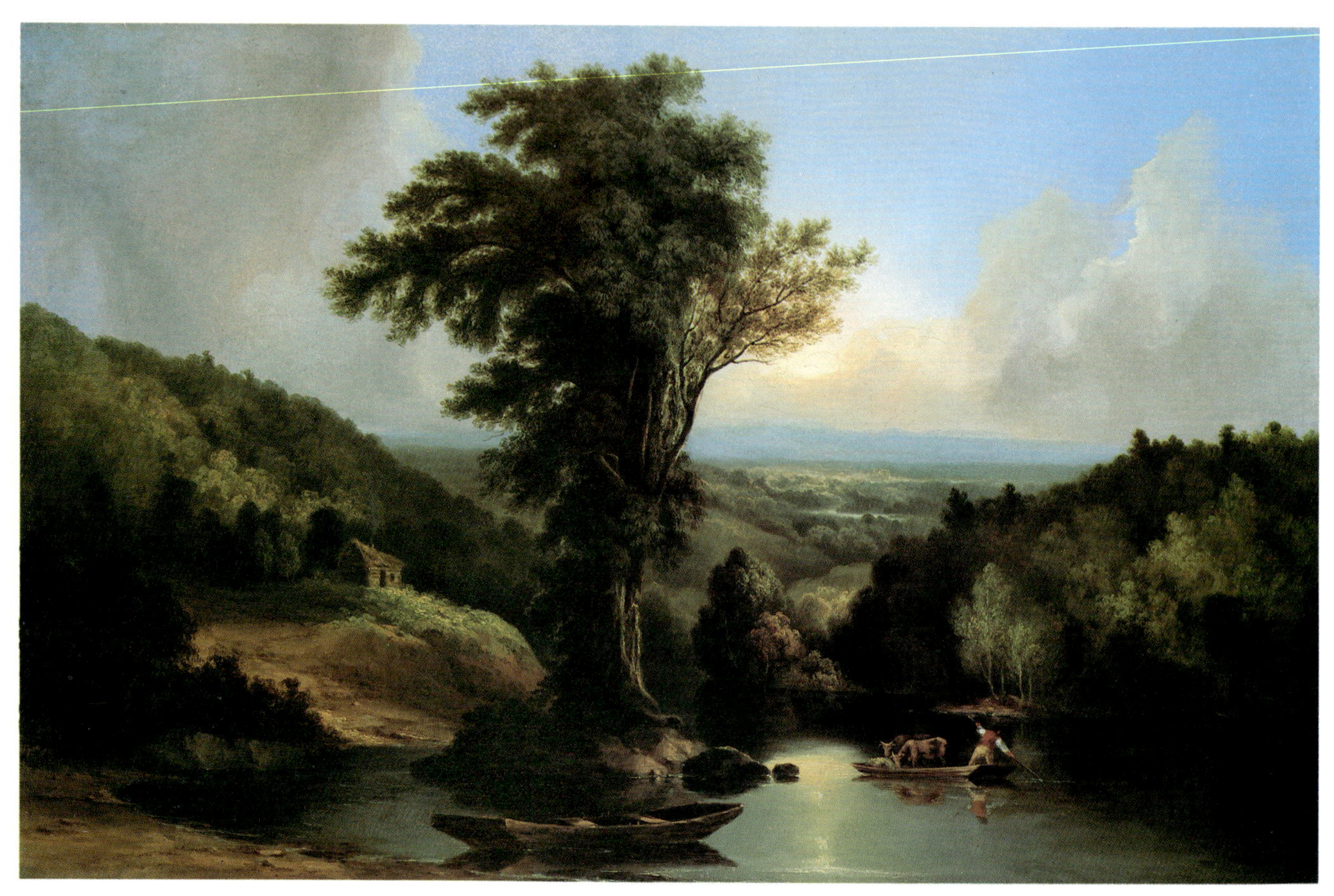

Thomas Doughty. *Landscape with Ferry*, ca. 1840 (no.32)

1. Hill, Shaw, introduction.

2. Ibid.

3. "The Land of the Lotos Eaters. Painted by R.S. Duncanson," *The Art-Journal* (London), N.S., v. 5 (1866), 93.

4. Many scholars have referred to this trans-atlantic cultural exchange in recent publications on American art, but to date no comprehensive treatment of the theme exists. For important groundwork on the subject see Flexner; Gerdts; Novak, 1980; Powell; Stein; and Sweet.

5. Anonymous [John Britton], *The Beauties of Wiltshire* (London, 1801-25), v. 2, 218; cited in Hayes, 1982, v. 1, 17.

6. Ibid., 17-18.

7. C.A. DuFresnoy, *The Art of Painting* (London, 1716); cited in Elizabeth G. Holt, ed., *Michelangelo and the Mannerists, the Baroque and the Eighteenth Century* (Garden City, 1958), 168.

8. Ibid., 167.

9. Ibid., 176.

10. Sir Joshua Reynolds, *Discourses on Art* (San Marino, 1959), 171.

11. Ibid., 160f.

12. Salvator Rosa (1615-73), the third great landscape painter in Italy in the 17th century, incorporated Biblical and mythological figures in highly expressive landscape settings. His painterly dynamism and emotionally-charged atmosphere and motifs had a great impact on the development of the sublime mode in British painting. Rosa was generally regarded as Claude's opposite, the painter of "savage and uncultivated nature;" see Manwaring, 1925.

13. Waterhouse, 1953, 172.

14. Reynolds, 70.

15. "On Landscape Painting," *The New York Weekly Magazine,* v. 59 (August 17, 1796), 49.

16. *Spring;* cited in Wilton, 1980b, 36.

17. James Thomson, Preface to *Winter* (London, 1726); cited in Parris, 75.

18. Wilton, 1980b, 25.

19. C.R. Leslie, *Memoirs of the Life of John Constable* (London, 1951), 15.

20. Hawes, 57.

21. Goldberg, 34.

22. Richard Payne Knight, *An Analytical Inquiry into the Principles of Taste* (London, 1805); cited in Wilton, 1980b, 10.

23. Marjorie Nicholson; Powell, February 1978; Hawes.

24. Hawes, 2.

25. William Mason, ed., *The Poems and Letters of Thomas Gray* (London, 1820), 62; cited in White, xviii.

26. Wilton, 1980a, 39.

27. Benedict Nicholson.

28. Burke (no. 21), 48.

29. Ibid., 83.

30. Hugh Blair, *Lectures on Rhetoric and Belles Lettres* (1839); cited in Edmund Burke, *A Philosophical Enquiry into the Origin of our Ideas of the Sublime and Beautiful* (London, 1958), 1xxxviii.

31. Benjamin West, *Discourses* (London, 1793), 8; cited in Evans, 40.

32. Allston to Henry Pickering, Boston, 23 November 1827; cited in Goldyne, 21.

33. Dunlap, v. 2, pt. 2, 461.

34. Noble, 12-13.

35. Ibid., 100.

36. McShine, 63.

37. Ibid., 65.

38. Parris, 15.

39. Noble, 110-11.

40. Novak, 1980, 228.

41. Howat, 1972, 32.

42. Brooks Memorial Art Gallery, *Sixty Paintings* (Memphis, 1966), 25.

43. Asher Durand, ''Letters on Landscape Painting,'' *The Crayon,* I (1855), 34-35, 97-98; cited in McCoubrey, 112.

44. *The New York Magazine or Literary Repository,* IV, no. XII (December 1793), 736-41; cited in Powell, March 1978, 110.

45. ''On a Taste for the Picturesque,'' *Monthly Magazine, XXX* (July 1800), 12.

46. Cole to Robert Gilmor, 25 December 1826; cited in Baltimore *Annual II,* 47.

47. Much has been written on the relations of American literature to landscape painting in the early 19th century. Three of the most comprehensive treatments of the subject are James T. Callow, *Kindred Spirits, Knickerbocker Writers and American Artists, 1807-1855* (Chapel Hill, 1967); Blake Nevius, *Cooper's Landscapes, An Essay on the Picturesque Vision* (Berkeley, 1976); Donald A. Ringe, *The Pictorial Mode, Space and Time in the Art of Bryant, Irving & Cooper* (Lexington, 1971).

48. Bayard Taylor, ''The Scenery of Pennsylvania,'' *The Home Book of the Picturesque: or American Scenery, Art, and Literature,* New York, 1852; reprint ed. (Gainesville, 1967), 102.

49. Indianapolis Museum of Art, *Catalogue of American Paintings* (Indianapolis, 1970), 85.

50. Journal entry, 8 July 1837; cited in Noble, 177.

51. Journal entry, 9 October 1838; cited in Noble, 201.

52. Price, 137.

53. Bermingham, 3-4.

54. McCoubrey, 107.

55. Talbot, 34.

56. Flexner, 56-57.

57. McCoubrey, 112.

58. Ringe (as in n. 47), 21.

59. McCoubrey, 102.

60. A.G.I., ''Examination of Burke's Theory of the Sublime'', *The Knickerbocker,* II (August 1833), 119.

61. Durand, ''Letters on Landscape Painting''; cited in McCoubrey, 112.

62. J. Gray Sweeney, *American Painting* (Muskegon, 1980), 62.

63. McShine, 72.

64. The most comprehensive treatment of luminism is *American Light, The Luminist Movement, 1850-1875, Paintings, Drawings, Photographs,* exhibition (New York, 1980).

65. *Selected Writings of Ralph Waldo Emerson,* ed. William H. Gilman (New York, 1965), 189.

66. Burke, 82.

67. Anthony Ashley Cooper, Earl of Shaftesbury, *Characteristics* (1711 and later); cited in Hussey, 53-54.

68. Letter from Church to Charles Parsons, April 23, 1883.

69. Ibid.

This checklist is divided into three sections according to three aesthetic theories: the beautiful, the picturesque, and the sublime. Works are listed chronologically with British preceding American artists. Height precedes width in measurements.

THE BEAUTIFUL

1. Richard Wilson (British, 1713-82). *Tivoli: Temple of the Sibyl and the Campagna* (1763-67), oil on canvas, 37 " × 49½ ". Memphis Brooks Museum of Art, Memphis, Tennessee, Gift of Mr. and Mrs. Morrie A. Moss.

From an early age Richard Wilson was attracted to classical art and literature. The son of a successful Anglican rector, he received a solid education in his Welsh home. Because of his mother's aristocratic connections, Wilson was sponsored to study portraiture in London in 1729. He later made a decent living from portraits and practiced this genre until he made his grand tour from 1750 to 1756. While in Italy he met Francesco Zuccarelli (1702-88) and Claude-Joseph Vernet (1714-89), two of Europe's most respected landscapists, who influenced his turn to landscape painting as a life's vocation. In Italy he sketched views and studied the contemporary and past masters of landscape. Upon his return to England he quickly established a reputation as the sole English master in the field of ideal landscape and the first Englishman to make a profession of landscape painting.[1]

He recreated many scenes recorded in his Italian sketchbooks into paintings in his London studio. When some compositions were popular and sold well, he would repeat them, often with variations, for a variety of patrons. Wilson affectionately termed these compositions "good breeders," and they were his primary source of income. *Tivoli: Temple of the Sibyl and the Campagna* (1763-67), one of his most frequently repeated subjects, exists in almost twenty variations.[2] Wilson painted the first of the series while in Rome in 1752.[3] The foreground of *Tivoli* is entirely imaginary and sets a stage for the figures who look into a landscape composed in the manner of Gaspard Dughet's *View of Ariccia* (The National Gallery, London).[4] The silhouetted tree, winding path, and hilltop city in both paintings are remarkably similar. David Solkin, however, has pinpointed a closer source in an early 18th-century disciple of Gaspard, l'Orizzonte (Jan Frans van Bloemen, 1662-1749). L'Orizzonte's *View of Tivoli* (private collection) records the town from exactly the same site as Wilson's.[5] Wilson's imaginary foreground with decaying tree trunk and fluidly expressive tree is much more rugged than l'Orizzonte's. In addition, Wilson replaced Gaspard's and l'Orizzonte's classically draped actors with a humble shepherd overlooking the work of a diligent artist.

1. Solkin.
2. Constable, 222-25.
3. Now in The National Gallery of Ireland, Dublin.
4. French, 19.
5. Solkin, 183.

2. Richard Wilson. *The White Monk*, oil on canvas, 28¼ × 36 ". Muskegon Museum of Art, Muskegon, Michigan.

3. George Barret (British, 1732?-84). *Landscape with Ruins* (ca. 1765), oil on canvas, 24 " × 36¼ ", Indianapolis Museum of Art, Indianapolis, Indiana, James E. Roberts Fund.

4. Charles Turner after Joseph M.W. Turner (British, 1775-1851). "The Bridge in the Middle Distance (The Sun Between the Trees)" (1808) from the *Liber Studiorum*, etching and mezzotint, image: 7⅛ " × 10⅜ ", 1st state. Indianapolis Museum of Art, Indianapolis, Indiana, Bequest of Kurt F. Pantzer, Sr.

5. Joseph M. W. Turner. "Junction of the Severn and the Wye" (1811) from the *Liber Studiorum*, etching and mezzotint, image: 7⅛ " × 10⅜ ", 1st state. Indianapolis Museum of Art, Indianapolis, Indiana, Bequest of Kurt F. Pantzer, Sr.

These two prints are early impressions from Turner's first major publishing project, the *Liber Studiorum* (1807-19). Issued in fourteen editions over a twelve-year period, the portfolio finally numbered seventy-one etchings and mezzotints of the hundred originally planned. The project was inspired by Richard Earlom's 1779 publication of Claude's *Liber Veritatis* in mezzotint engravings. The *Liber Veritatis* was a collection of sepia wash drawings Claude Lorrain created to document all of his paintings. With his *Liber Studiorum*, Turner attempted to rival Claude and the masters by offering a large number and variety of landscape styles, moods, and compositions. Turner etched each plate from existing or newly-conceived designs. He then turned the plates over to craftsmen to add rich tones with their mezzotint rockers. In order to differen-

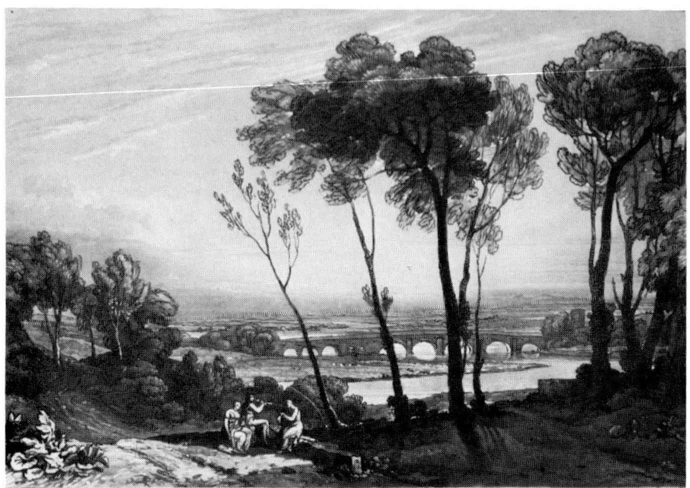

Charles Turner after Joseph M.W. Turner. "The Bridge in the Middle Distance," 1808, *Liber Studiorum* (no. 4)

tiate the subject of each print, Turner created a classification system of initials at the top of each work: A for architectural, H for historical, M for mountains or marines, Ms for mountainous sublime, P for pastoral, and EP for elevated pastoral.[1]

"The Bridge in the Middle Distance" is annotated EP and directly reflects Claude's example. A trio of classically draped figures leads the eye into the landscape along a series of diagonals to the river, past the bridge, and on to the luminous horizon. The enframing trees and arched bridge are stock motifs in the Claudian repertoire and reinforce a mood of pastoral beauty. In her study of English landscape symbolism, Adele Holcomb remarks that "Turner...rarely evoked Claude without employing this motif" of the arched bridge.[2] "The Junction of the Severn and the Wye," a slightly later design, beautifully defines Turner's application of Claudian formulas to English scenery. He transfers the composition, with enframing trees and diagonals leading to the softly lit sky, from the earlier print, while the inclusion of a traveller resting in the foreground and medieval English ruins identify the locale. Although this site was a popular stop on tours of the picturesque, Turner transforms it into a serenely calm idyll. Turner here carries into another generation Wilson's vision of an English landscape suited to ideals of classical beauty.

Because of their mass production, easy transportation, and relatively low costs, the prints of the *Liber Studiorum* were known and circulated in America shortly after their publication. Americans' awareness of the prints was rather scanty early in the century, but by 1850 knowledge of Turner's reputation and the *Liber Studiorum* was widespread. Early in the century the Royal Academy president Benjamin West had recommended Turner's paintings to his American students and visitors, such as Washington Allston, who in turn advised Thomas Cole to study Turner: "Turner's 'Liber Studiorum' would be a most useful work for him to possess."[3]

In America Turner's works were known mostly through mezzotints and illustrated books. The first Turner painting to find a home in America was *Staffa, Fingal's Cave* (1831, Yale Center for British Art), purchased in 1845, sight unseen, by James Lenox of New York. The painting, which "appeared to him indistinct throughout,"[4] confused Lenox, as it did most Americans who saw it. For Americans accustomed to the linear nature of Turner's mezzotints, their first encounter with the broadly handled, boldly colored paintings was a shock. Cole, like other American artists who saw Turner's work in the flesh, appreciated his earlier works much more than the later, more painterly ones. Cole described the later paintings as "splendid combinations of colour. But they are destitute of all appearance of solidity: all appears transparent and soft, and reminds one of jellies and confection."[5] Due to this bias for linear details, Turner's influence on the Hudson River School is largely limited to the qualities of scale and dynamism in his works rather than their specific handling. Despite that, several comparisons can be found in this exhibition, such as those between Turner's *Liber* print "Little Devil's Bridge" (1809, no. 39) and Jacob Ward's *Natural Bridge* (ca. 1835, no. 48), and "Ben Arthur, Scotland" (1819, no. 40) and Frederic Church's *Mount Desert Island, Maine* (1865, no. 59).

1. See *Liber Studiorum by J. M. W. Turner* (New York: Charles Scribner's Sons, n.d.) and Wilton, 87-89.
2. Adele Holcomb. "The Bridge in the Middle Distance: Symbolic Elements in Romantic Landscape," *Art Quarterly*, v. 37, no. 1 (Spring 1974), 31-58.
3. Goldyne, 12, 21.
4. Ibid., 26-27.
5. Ibid., 23.

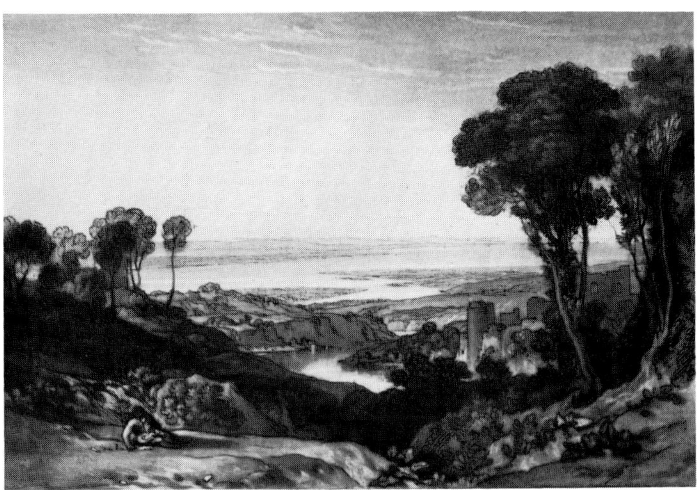

Joseph M.W. Turner. "The Junction of the Severn and the Wye," 1811, *Liber Studiorum* (no.5)

6. Charles A. DuFresnoy (French, 1611-68). *The Art of Painting.* Translated by William Mason. (York: Printed by A. Ward, 1783). Washington University, The John M. Olin Library, St. Louis, Missouri.

7. Sir Joshua Reynolds (British, 1723-92). *The Works of Sir Joshua Reynolds.* (London: Printed for T. Cadell, 1798). Washington University, Art and Architecture Library, St. Louis, Missouri.

8. J.T. Willmore after Samuel Prout (British, 1784-1852). Sibyl's Temple, Tivoli" from *Views of Cities and Scenery in Italy, France and Switzerland,* v. I (London-Paris-New York: 1836). Washington University, Art and Architecture Library, St. Louis, Missouri.

9. Thomas Cole (American, 1801-48). *Landscape Composition, Italian Scenery (1833),* oil on canvas, 37½ " × 54½ ". The New-York Historical Society, New York, New York.

As Henry Tuckerman pointed out in 1867, to Cole "may be directly traced the primal success of landscape painting as a national art in the New World."[1] In his double career as a specialist in wilderness subjects and a painter of allegory and history, Cole epitomized the romantic spirit in early 19th-century American art.

In 1825 his paintings of Catskill and Hudson River scenery were discovered in a picture dealer's window by John Trumbull, president of the American Academy of Fine Arts, who then introduced Cole to the leading artists and writers in New York. Cole quickly aligned himself with the intellectual movement seeking to establish a uniquely American national culture. His paintings of the untamed wilderness may be seen as artistic counterparts to the celebration of American nature in the writings of Cooper, Bryant, and Irving. Like Wilson in Britain a half-century earlier, he established an inspiring example for future American landscape painters through his life-long dedication to the art. The originality, moral fiber, and popular acclaim of Cole's landscapes assured the increasing prominence of landscape paintings in the annual exhibitions of American academies.

Cole was distinguished from most of his contemporaries for the breadth of his aspirations. Not content simply to record the majestic wilderness, he aspired to excel in the painting of allegorical and philosophically oriented compositions, the highest pursuits of the artist. This landscape composition was painted in 1833 for Luman Reed, the New York merchant who also commissioned Cole's five-part allegorical cycle *The Course of Empire* (1833-36, The New-York Historical Society).[2] Cole had just returned from three years of study in Europe, where in addition to absorbing the works of Claude Lorrain at London's National Gallery, he had also nurtured an empassioned response to Italian scenery. In numerous Italian landscapes of the 1830s Cole combined imaginary and observed landscape elements in compositions firmly linked to the classical tradition of Claude and Poussin. In this amalgam of panorama and pastoral, a giant Italian pine anchors the design at the left side. It oversees a vast landscape that features a composite of the round Temple of the Sibyl at Tivoli, an aqueduct, and the Lake of Nemi. Such monuments were standard stops on the grand tour and had been painted by Wilson (no.1). While in England Cole had made only one copy of a British painting, "a pastoral scene by Wilson, whose truthfulness to nature he admired."[3] Cole's attention to effects of light and atmosphere in this Italian landscape recall Wilson's vision of harmony and repose. The diminutive figures in the foreground contrast a group of dancing peasants at the base of the tree to a solitary thinker stretched out against the broken column. They seem to symbolize Cole's reactions to Italian landscape: entranced by the beauty of the countryside, especially by the golden softness of its light,[4] he was also struck by the land's associations with man's "mortal triumph and defeat. . . In the crumbling ruins beneath the mantle of the seasons, lay the bones of empire."[5]

1. Tuckerman, 225.
2. Richard J. Koke, *American Landscape and Genre Paintings in the New York Historical Society* (New York & Boston, 1982), v. 1, 189-90.
3. Noble, 76.
4. Letter from Cole to Gilmor, Florence, 29 January 1832; cited in Baltimore *Annual II*, 74.
5. Noble, 110-11.

10. Thomas Doughty (American, 1793-1856). *Anthony's Nose, Lake George, N.Y.* (1837-38), oil on canvas 30 " × 42 1/8 ". Memphis Brooks Museum of Art, Memphis, Tennessee, Memphis Park Commission Purchase.

11. Samuel L. Gerry (American, 1813-91). *Lake of the Avernus* (1851), oil on canvas, 27 1/8 " × 37 3/16 ". Museum of Art and Archaeology, University of Missouri, Columbia, Missouri.

Samuel Lancaster Gerry, one of Boston's leading landscape painters, became a specialist in depicting the White Mountains of New Hampshire. As in the case of nearly every Hudson River School painter, he made the pilgrimage to Europe, traveling and sketching in England, France, Switzerland, and Italy in 1837-40 and again in 1850-54.[1] While in Italy he painted a serene composition of the *Lake of the Avernus* (1851) which reveals the impact of his encounter with the classical landscape tradition.[2] Elegantly attenuated trees rise majestically into a brilliant sky. As in Cole's *Italian Scenery* (no. 9), and the works of Claude and other classical painters, the landscape contains a cliff-like rise in the middleground bearing a classical ruin and overlooking a tranquil body of water surrounded by irregular hills. The sky floods a large part of the scene in brilliant golden light, providing a poignant contrast to the heavily-shadowed foreground. A shepherd leaning on his staff, his resting flock, and the serene calm of the landscape, contribute to a sense of arcadian perfection, an idyll of pastoral repose. The figure of the old monk, a classical symbol of peace of mind,[3] sits amidst the ruins of ancient civilization. Man here exists in peaceful harmony with the timeless patterns of nature.

1. William H. Gerdts, *Revealed Masters, 19th Century American Art*, exhibition (American Federation of Arts, New York, 1974), 11f; cited in Hallenberg, 52.
2. Roethlisberger, in *Im Licht von Claude Lorrain* (1983), argues

for an identification of the Lake of Nemi as the painting's subject.
3. Hallenberg, 55.

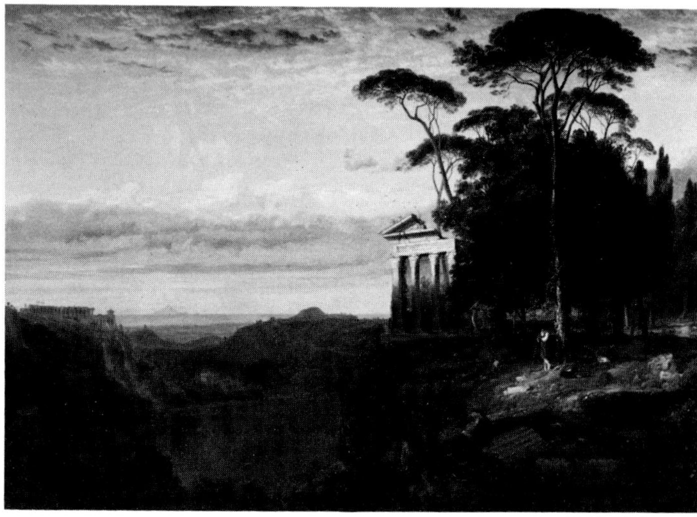

Samuel L. Gerry. *Lake of the Avernus*, 1851 (no.11)

12. George Inness (American, 1825-94). *The Close of Day* (1863), oil on canvas, 25 " × 35 ". The J.B. Speed Art Museum, Louisville, Kentucky.

13. Asher B. Durand (American, 1796-1886). *Landscape, A Peaceful Day, Sunset* (1870), oil on canvas, 14 1/4 " × 24 1/8 ". Washington University Gallery of Art, St. Louis, Missouri, Gift of Charles Parsons, 1905.

The St. Louis collector Samuel A. Coale, Jr., acquired this painting from Durand in 1870, after having previously bought one of his "inimitable tree truths, with a bit of charming foreground, and as much of God's atmosphere and sky as you can spare."[1] The latter, shown at the 1869 St. Louis Fair, "elicited much praise,"[2] and Durand, eager to follow up on this success, sent Coale what he felt was "one of my best," so as "to have a more complete specimen of my work in the West than the unpretending study of nature you possess."[3] Where the earlier picture may have been one of Durand's characteristic forest compositions, filled with intricately described natural detail, the later piece is a generalized pastoral scene. The painting translates into rustic American terms the mellow and harmonious nature seen in Wilson's Italian views and Turner's English idylls.

Late in his career, Durand returned to the classical tradition that had initially marked his emergence as a landscape painter in the 1830s. He abandoned his earlier concentration on a detailed rendering of nature for a broad treatment of landscape forms and moods. Here, a peaceful day is laid out through a rolling vista of sun-flecked hills and misty groves of trees. Durand's painting, an idealized vision of domesticated American nature, reflects an attitude that was peculiarly American in its synthesis of aesthetic sentiment and morality. William Cullen Bryant (1794-1878)

expressed that reverence towards God's presence in the landscape in these lines from "A Forest Hymn":

Be it ours to meditate,
In these calm shades, thy milder majesty,
And to the beautiful order of thy works
Learn to conform the order of our lives.[4]

1. Letter from Coale to Durand, St. Louis, 5 August 1869 (New York Public Library); cited in Lawall, 1978, 151.
2. Coale to Durand, St. Louis, 18 July 1870 (New York Public Library); ibid., 152.
3. Durand to Coale, South Orange, N.J., 21 July 1870 (New-York Historical Society); ibid., 153.
4. Cited in Lawall, 1971, 67.

THE PICTURESQUE

14. Thomas Gainsborough (British, 1727-88). *View in Suffolk* (ca. 1755), oil on canvas, 37″ × 49½″. The Saint Louis Art Museum, St. Louis, Missouri, Bequest of Cora Liggett Fowler.

Although his reputation initally grew from his fashionable portraits, Gainsborough was the first native artist to sustain a vision of landscape painting as a reflection of rural England. Born in the farming town of Sudbury, Gainsborough evinced an amazing talent for drawing at an early age. He was reputed to have forged notes to relieve himself of school responsiblities so that he could sketch the surrounding countryside.[1] Much later in life he proclaimed that his childhood in "Suffolk made me an artist."[2] After he arrived in London in 1740, he apprenticed with the French engraver Hubert Gravelot (1669-1773) and restored and copied Dutch landscapes, then becoming popular in the English art market.[3] There he developed an awareness of the French rococo and Dutch landscape styles that were to direct the course of his painting for the next forty years. In Suffolk during the 1750s he created a large number of landscapes of sandy banked rivers peopled with the rustic peasants of the area. Patronage, however, was limited, and in 1759 he moved on to the resort town of Bath, where his reputation blossomed as a portrait painter.[4] Gainsborough's success in this genre earned him widespread critical appreciation and a handsome income. Though he enjoyed the fashionable life, he longed for the bliss of a country existence. He confessed that "I'm sick of portraits and wish very much to take my Viola da Gamba and walk off to some sweet village where

I can paint landskips and enjoy the Fag End of Life in quietness and ease."[5]

Gainsborough's fondness for a leisurely rural life permeates his Suffolk landscapes. In this *View in Suffolk* (ca. 1755) he synthesizes a sentimental view of peasant life with an imaginary landscape full of dynamic flourishes. The charming motifs of the horse and dog drinking at the river, the peasants courting, and the cow bellowing enliven the scene. No evidence of farm labor appears, and everyone is relaxed or at rest. This is an idealized vision of peasant life without the pains and hardships actually known by the lowest social class of 18th-century England. The view features several elements typical of Gainsborough's work during this period. The shy girl coyly turning from the courting youth reoccurs in many paintings of this time and reveals Gainsborough's awareness of the French rococo tradition. Among his repertoire of landscape forms, the sandy river banks, craggy middleground tree, and burdock leaves distinguish his works of this period and result from an early exposure to 17th-century Dutch landscape painters. In its unique depiction of English rural life and synthesis of Dutch and French elements, this painting is very accomplished for a young man of twenty-three.

1. Hayes, 1982, 40.
2. Geoffrey Williamson, *The Ingenious Mr. Gainsborough* (London, 1972), 14.
3. John Hayes, *The Drawings of Thomas Gainsborough* (New Haven, 1971), 2.

4. Waterhouse, 1958, 19-20.
5. Letter of 1767 to William Jackson; see Woodall, 115, no. 56.

15. Paul Sandby (British, 1730-1809). *Landscape with Tree, Tower and Mountain* (ca. 1790), watercolor, 10" × 12½". The Sheldon Swope Art Gallery, Terre Haute, Indiana.

16. Philip J. de Loutherbourg (British, 1740-1812). *Wooded Landscape with Figures*, oil on canvas, 17" × 21⅛". Washington University Gallery of Art, St. Louis, Missouri.

De Loutherbourg had an enthusiasm for a diverse range of styles and subject matter. Raised in a Germanic family of painters and trained in Paris under the history painter Francesco-Giuseppe Casanova (1727-1802), de Loutherbourg was versed in European art and was particularly familiar with the 17th-century Dutch masters. By the time he arrived in London in 1771, he had achieved pre-eminence in France as an academician and *peintre du roi*. His first steady employment in England was as the stage designer for the Drury Lane Theater through the invitation of David Garrick, the premier dramatic actor in England. From these auspicious beginnings, de Loutherbourg's wandering brush led him to paint shipwrecks, *banditi*, landscapes, theatrical panoramas, and battle scenes. His last major position was as the history painter to the Duke of Gloucester in 1808.[1]

Throughout de Loutherbourg's various shifts in style and subjects, he consistently worked in the landscape genre, and, during his first decade in England, he painted many rural idylls under the influence of the Dutch and his associate, Thomas Gainsborough. This lively and humourous example typifies his work in this picturesque manner. The anxious fellow in the foreground has dropped his hat on the path in his haste to wrap his arms around the young maiden. The curious donkeys and dogs watch with amusing anticipation, while off to the left sit a woman and child, unaware of the amorous activity under the bower of arched trees. He sets all of this excitement into a sumptuously verdant forest interior.

The history of the painting is quite as lively as the anecdote it portrays. It was originally accessioned as a landscape by de Loutherbourg, but in 1965 that attribution was questioned by the art historian John Hayes. At that time Mr. Hayes noticed that this painting was a replication of a landscape on loan to the Gainsborough House, Sudbury. C.H. Collins Baker, former Keeper of the National Gallery in London, first assigned the hand of Gainsborough to the Sudbury picture in 1951. Based on a comparison with paintings by Pierre Norblin de la Gourdaine (1745-1830), Mr. Hayes reattributed both paintings to this artist, who, like de Loutherbourg, was a former pupil of Casanova. The resemblances between the St. Louis and Sudbury paintings are remarkable down to the details of rendering in the branches and leaves. All of the figures, animals, and trees are in the same positions and proportions in both paintings. To compound the problem, the St. Louis painting received a cleaning in 1969 that revealed a signature in the path, "P.J. de Louther...," which appears to be contemporary with the remainder of the painting.

A comparison of the *Wooded Landscape with Figures*, especially in the dappled touch used to render the leaves, makes an attribution to de la Gourdaine difficult. De la Gourdaine's leaves tend to be thin, broad washes of fan-shaped forms in a French rococo manner. The style of the de Loutherbourg painting is much closer to Gainsborough's early paintings and prints of wooded landscapes with gypsies. De Loutherbourg's friendship with Gainsborough would substantiate this stylistic relationship. However, de Loutherbourg was not known to imitate Gainsborough, as in the Sudbury painting originally attributed to Gainsborough.[2] Perhaps a closer examination of the Sudbury painting will reveal de Loutherbourg's signature and alleviate this stylistic and attribution problem.

1. Joppien.
2. Hayes, 1982, v. 1, 237-93.

17. William Gilpin (British, 1724-1804). *Landscape with River Valley*, pen and ink over pencil and sepia wash, 10 ¹¹/₁₆" × 14³/₈". Indianapolis Museum of Art, Indianapolis, Indiana.

18. William Gilpin. *Observations on the River Wye*, 2nd edition. (London: 1789). University of Iowa, Special Collections, Iowa City, Iowa.

19. William Gilpin. *Three Essays: On the Picturesque, On Picturesque Travel, and On Sketching Landscape.* (London: 1792). University of Iowa, Special Collections, Iowa City, Iowa.

20. Joseph M.W. Turner. *Matlock* (1794), tinted wash and watercolor, 4" × 6³/₈". Indianapolis Museum of Art, Indianapolis, Indiana, gift in memory of Dr. and Mrs. Hugo O. Pantzer by their Children.

21. After Thomas Hearne (British, 1744-1817). ''Picturesque and Improved Landscapes'' from Richard Payne Knight (British, 1750-1824), *The Landscape, a Didactic Poem.* (London: 1794). Washington University, The John M. Olin Library, St. Louis, Missouri.

22. John Crome (British, 1768-1821). *Landscape* (ca. 1809), oil on canvas, 20¼ " × 24½ ". Washington University Gallery of Art, St. Louis, Missouri, Gift of Charles Parsons, 1905.

John Crome was the primary motivator behind the thriving regional group of landscape painters known as the Norwich School. He was born to a poor journeyman weaver. At the age of fourteen he was apprenticed for seven years to a house-, sign-, and coach-painter.[1] From these humble beginnings, Crome rose to prominence in Norfolk where he became the leading drawing master. In 1790 Thomas Harvey, a collector and patron of the arts in Norwich, allowed the painter access to his large collection, and this initial exposure to English and continental masters affected the subsequent course of Crome's career. Three paintings in Harvey's collection were especially influential for Crome's artistic development: Thomas Gainsborough's *The Cottage Door* (The Huntington Library, San Marino, Ca.), Richard Wilson's *View of Baiae* (present whereabouts unknown), and Meindert Hobbema's *Landscape* (Buehrle Collection, Zurich).[2]

Stylistic motifs from these three sources are readily identifiable in this *Landscape*, datable to around 1809. In his pioneering American publications on Crome and the Norwich School, Norman L. Goldberg identifies this painting as one of two exhibited at the Crome Memorial Exhibition in Norwich in 1821 as *Compositions in the Style of Wilson.*[3] The rich green and brown tonality, contrasted to the steely blue sky, does refer to Wilson. Hobbema's influence is seen in the intimate forest scene, encompassing a group of cows watering at the river and boys playing along the bank. The thickly textured tree bark and interest in rural English scenery descends from Gainsborough's early paintings. The Gainsborough painting Crome saw in Thomas Harvey's collection, however, was a late ''fancy piece,'' created with fluid dashes of pigment, not in the tight style evidenced in this *Landscape*. All factors considered, this scene admirably represents a combination of source material that is at the root of English landscape painting.

1. Norman Goldberg, *Landscapes of the Norwich School*, exhibition (Cummer Gallery of Art, 1967), 64.

2. Ibid., 23.
3. Ibid., 66, no. 3; Goldberg, 1978, 187, no. 36.

23. David Cox (British, 1783-1859). *Landscape with Hay Cart*, oil on canvas, 16¼ " × 24¼ ". Washington University Gallery of Art, St. Louis, Missouri, Acquisition of 1970.

24. Sir Uvedale Price (British, 1747-1829). *On the Picturesque: with an essay on the origins of taste, and much original matter, by Sir Thomas Dick Lauder, Bart.* Illustrations by Montagu Stanley. (Edinburgh: Caldwell, Lloyd, 1842). Washington University, Art and Architecture Library, St. Louis, Missouri.

25. Benjamin West (American, 1738-1820). *Woodcutters in Windsor Park* (1795), oil on canvas, 28" × 36". Indianapolis Museum of Art, Indianapolis, Indiana; Gift of Mrs. Nicholas H. Noyes.

Born near Swarthmore, Pennsylvania, Benjamin West rose to prominence in the field of history painting and succeeded Sir Joshua Reynolds as the second President of the Royal Academy. During his stay in Italy in 1760-63, the young artist became interested in the neoclassical revival of ancient art. After settling in London in 1763, West quickly established himself as a painter of large-scale figural compositions with subjects from ancient and modern history. A founding member of the Royal Academy, he promoted the ''grand style'' of Reynolds into the first decades of the 19th century.[1]

West painted very few landscapes, of which this is an important example. Commissioned by the Royal House, the painting documents the landscaping of Windsor Park, with woodcutters clearing trees for an unobstructed view of the Queen's lodge. This is a unique treatment of estate portraiture, synthesizing it with picturesque landscape gardening and placing the main subject in the distance. The focus is on the landscape itself and the laborers working it into a shapely park. Treatises on landscape gardening were prevalent at the time, and writers such as Sir Uvedale Price, Richard Payne Knight, and Humphrey Repton were stressing the natural and picturesque style in gardening. William Gilpin, the first major writer on the picturesque, was West's cousin, suggesting that West had close ties to the theorists and ideas of the picturesque. In its intimate view of rough forest scenery and the labors of men tied to the land, West's painting also relates to the rustic landscapes of Gainsborough and de Loutherbourg (nos. 14 & 16).

1. Evans.

26. Joshua Shaw (American, ca. 1777-1860). *Landscape with Cattle* (1818), oil on canvas, 31″ × 41″. The Butler Institute of American Art, Youngstown, Ohio.

Joshua Shaw was an important transitional figure in the development of American landscape painting. He exhibited landscapes, portraits, and still lifes at the Royal Academy from 1802 until 1817, when he emigrated to the United States, bringing a knowledge of contemporary British landscape styles and aesthetics. One of his earliest American landscapes, *Landscape with Cattle* is essentially a picturesque composition, shorn of the enframing trees and rough silhouettes. It can be compared to *Matlock* (1794, no. 20), an early watercolor by Turner, which Shaw may have known through the engraving after it published in the *Copper-Plate Magazine* (1795).[1] In both compositions the gently bowed stone bridge in the middleground echoes the massive background hill. The bridge's reflection in the still water and the groups of buildings fronting the river appear also in both pictures, indicating the pervasiveness of this compositional formula in British landscape painting. The mixture of cattle on a patch of pasture and a sweeping mountain range suggests Gilpin's concept of picturesque beauty as a balance of "the grand and the rural,"[2] a blend of sublime scale and pastoral repose. Above all, the light plays a dominant role in this presentation of the picturesque American countryside, light that immerses the sky and dissolves the distant vista and mountaintop.

1. Wilton, 1979, 311, no. 91.
2. William Gilpin, "Instructions for Examining Landscape," 2-4 (Ms. in Fitzwilliam Museum, Cambridge); cited in Barbier, 112-13.

27. John Hill after Joshua Shaw. "View on the North River, N.Y." from *Picturesque Views of American Scenery*, hand-colored etching and aquatint, plate: 15″ × 11$^7/_8$″, 1st state. (Philadelphia: 1820-21). The New-York Historical Society, New York, New York.

28. John Hill after Joshua Shaw. "Passaic River, Below the Falls" from *Picturesque Views of American Scenery*, hand-colored etching and aquatint, plate: 11$^7/_8$″ × 15″, 1st state. (Philadephia: 1820-21). The New-York Historical Society, New York, New York.

29. Attributed to Thomas Cole. *Romantic River Scene* (ca. 1820-22), charcoal on marble dust paper, 8¾″ × 11¾″. Collection of Mr. and Mrs. J. Gray Sweeney, Grand Rapids, Michigan.

30. Joshua Shaw. *The Pioneers* (ca. 1838), oil on canvas, 19″ × 27″, Indianapolis Museum of Art, Indianapolis, Indiana, James E. Roberts and Emma Harter Sweetser Funds.

Shaw's *The Pioneers* illustrates an incident from the settling of the New World, using the Delaware Water Gap as a scenic backdrop. Earlier renditions of the Water Gap, such as fellow Philadelphian Thomas Doughty's 1826 view, concentrated on the sublime scale and breathtaking beauty of the country as seen from a high vantage point.[1] Shaw elaborated the rugged profiles of the overlapping mountains to create a romantic background that features a castle-like ruin on one rise and overhead a flurry of cottony clouds. In contrast to his earlier *Landscape with Cattle* (no. 26), the foreground is essentially a platform or stage for the picturesque incident of frontiersmen cutting up a dead tree. The figure with raised axe is remarkably similar to a worker in Benjamin West's *Woodcutters in Windsor Park* (no. 25), a connection interesting in the light of Shaw's study under West in London.[2] The juxtaposition of the fallen trunk with a craggy tree recalls Gainsborough's use of these picturesque motifs in the foreground of the *View in Suffolk* (no. 14). This mixture of panoramic breadth and elegant vignette marked Shaw's landscapes of the 1830s and 40s, and, though he never was regarded with the same esteem as Cole or Durand, he did maintain a respectable position as a landscape painter with such generalized evocations of American scenery.

1. Private collection; see Goodyear, 23.
2. Anthony Janson discusses an interesting comparison to contemporary British landscapes in the *Indianapolis Museum of Art Handbook of European and American Paintings to 1945* (Indianapolis, 1981).

31. Thomas Cole. *Sunset in the Catskills* (1841), oil on canvas, 22½″ × 30¼″. Museum of Fine Arts, Boston, Massachusetts, Bequest of Mary Fuller Wilson.

32. Thomas Doughty. *Landscape with Ferry* (ca. 1840), oil on canvas, 26¾″ × 41$^1/_8$″. The Nelson Atkins Museum of Art, Kansas City, Missouri, Nelson Fund.

William Dunlap wrote in 1834, "Mr. Doughty has long stood in the first rank as a landscape painter — he was at one time the first and best in the country."[1] Though subsequent critical attention has focused on the pioneer efforts of Cole and Durand, Doughty preceded both as the first native-born artist to devote himself to American landscape subjects. The Philadelphia painter turned from an early career as a leather currier to landscape painting about 1820 and quickly established himself as a master of small-scale, realistic views of country estates and scenery of the Northeast. He appears to have been mostly self-taught, although he later copied Dutch and Italian paintings in the collection of his patron, Robert Gilmor.[2] After gaining a solid reputation in Philadelphia, Doughty moved to Boston in 1832, where the demand for his quiet, lyrical landscapes was so great that he would produce multiple versions of certain formulaic pieces.[3] In the 1840s his art fell out of favor with critics who stressed the "truth to nature" characteristic of Durand's close-up studies of isolated woodland elements.

Doughty is the pre-eminent American painter of picturesque nature, and his canvases bear marks of his admiration for the English picturesque tradition. He may have derived some intimacy with the genre from his Philadelphia neighbor, Joshua Shaw, whose *Picturesque Views of American Scenery* was published at about the same time as Doughty's debut. *Landscape with Ferry* has been dated to ca. 1840[4], after Doughty's brief trip to Britain (1837-38). The broadly symmetrical design centered on a handsomely silhouetted tree recalls Claude Lorrain's pastoral landscapes, such as the painting of ca. 1637 (North Carolina Museum of Art, Raleigh) then in the collection of Lord Northwick.[5] Doughty created a more specifically Claudian composition in *Anthony's Nose, Lake George* (no. 10), painted while in London. In that painting, the light is a generalized golden brown, and the vast spreading tree at left introduces the diagonal recession into space. In the Nelson *Landscape* Doughty achieved a balance between observation of nature and adherence to classical composition; the mellow tones of the partially illuminated hills and the silvery sheen of the still lake reveal a sensitive attention to the character of American landscape. The eye is free to meander along the lazy outlines of the river banks leading to the undulating vista of low hills on the horizon. As an emblem of the vitality of this rich landscape, a solitary tree with many branches rises majestically between the receding slopes. The empty ferryboat in the foreground, directly below the tree, provides a silent association to man's congenial relations to nature. Cropsey made similar use of an abandoned boat in the foreground of *The Hudson at Piermont* (no. 35).

1. Dunlap, v. 2, pt. 2, 381.
2. Goodyear, 15.
3. Ibid., 17.
4. Ibid., 29, no. 40.
5. Marcel Roethlisberger, *Claude Lorrain, The Paintings* (New Haven: 1961), 138-39.

33. John F. Kensett. *Landscape* (1840s), oil on canvas, 12″ × 10¹/₈″. Washington Univerisity Gallery of Art, St. Louis, Missouri, Gift of Charles Parsons, 1905.

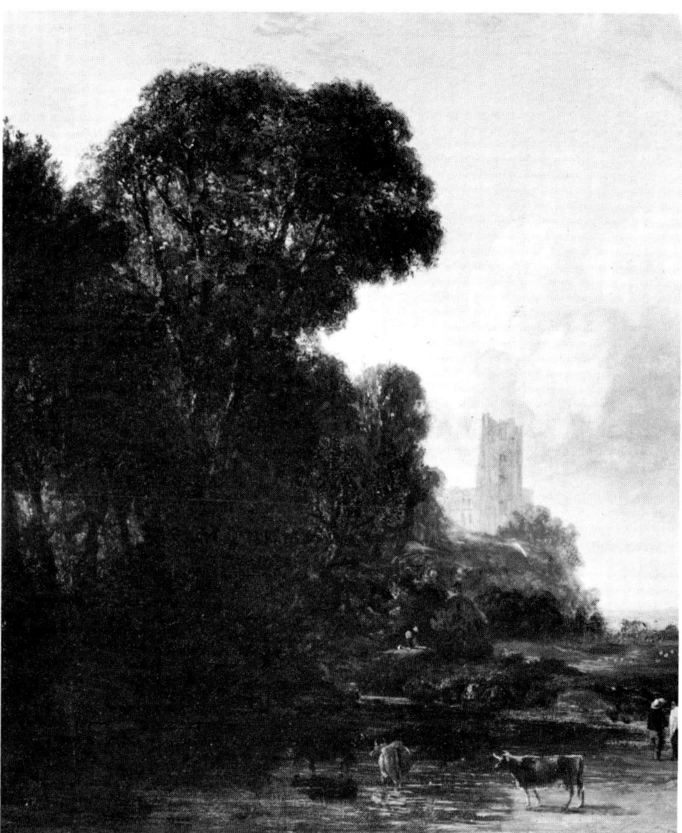

John F. Kensett. *Landscape*, 1840s (no.33)

34. Asher B. Durand. *Woodland Landscape*, oil on canvas, 23½ " × 16⅞". The Saint Louis Art Museum, St. Louis, Missouri, Gift of John Allan Love in memory of his wife, Mary Potter Love.

35. Jasper F. Cropsey (American, 1823-1900). *The Hudson at Piermont* (1852), oil on canvas, 60" × 48⅜". The Saint Louis Art Museum, St. Louis, Missouri, Gift of John Allan Love in memory of his wife, Mary Potter Love.

After a youthful career as an architect, Cropsey turned to landscape painting in the mid-1840s, having earlier copied in oils engravings of Claude's works.[1] Cropsey's name became synonymous with the inspired painting of the American autumn, and it is a tribute to his skill that when British audiences encountered his massive *Autumn on the Hudson River* (1860, National Gallery of Art, Washington, D.C.), they could not believe that such vivid colors were based on reality.[2] Like his contemporary Frederic Church, Cropsey emphasized moral content in his landscapes, but rather than travel to exotic sites for subjects, he rooted himself in the Northeast and painted the forests in autumn splendor. Cropsey inherited from Thomas Cole a deep appreciation of the picturesque variety and associational power of forest scenes. In addition, his woodland subjects of the 1850s and 60s exhibit an understanding of the expressive capacity of trees that can be linked to British writings on the picturesque.

The Hudson at Piermont puts far into the background the scene of the title, the thin spit of land extending out into the river, where steamboats docked to connect passengers from New York to New Jersey.[3] In keeping with the British picturesque format, the foreground displays meticulously detailed natural effects — the fall of light on the bow of the empty rowboat, the rough textures of rock and ground, isolated plants rendered with botanical accuracy. The focal subject of the painting is the contrast of a pair of trees silhouetted against the vast sunny sky. With moist, dense pigments reminiscent of Gainsborough, Cropsey delineates the different characteristics of these trees, suggesting a contrast of "picturesque" to "beautiful" nature. In his "Essay on American Scenery" (1836), Cole had written that "trees are like men, differing widely in character; in sheltered spots, or under the influence of culture, they show few contrasting points...But in exposed situations, wild and uncultivated, battling with the elements and with one another for the possession of a morsel of soil...they exhibit striking peculiarities, and sometimes original grandeur."[4] One tree is scarred by the effects of weather (lightning) and man's exploitation (the cut branch), while the other is taller, younger, and unmarred. Price also discussed the differences among trees, terming a beautiful tree one of graceful and elegant proportions, lofty height, and "fresh, tender foliage and bark," while a picturesque tree exhibits effects of age and decay, as when some limbs are shattered or a broken stump is left, and proportions are short, thick, and irregular.[5] By offering the trees as emblems of the stages of life, Cropsey found a way of merging the close observation of nature stressed by Durand with romantic metaphors. Autumn in the American forest is presented as an intermingling of life and death in a coloristic blaze of poignant beauty.

   1. Bermingham, 30.
   2. Ibid., 7.
   3. Talbot.
   4. Thomas Cole, "Essay on American Scenery," *The American Monthly Magazine*, New Series, v. 1 (January 1836), 1-12; cited in McCoubrey, 107.
   5. Price (no. 24), 94.

THE SUBLIME

36. John Robert Cozens (British, 1752-97). *Between Chamonix and Martigny* (1776), tinted drawing, 9⅜" × 14⅛". Yale Center for British Art, New Haven Connecticut, Paul Mellon Collection.

The expressive power of this tinted drawing transcends the cool, grey-green tonality that first impresses the viewer. Cozens executed this subtle work on his first grand tour of Europe under the sponsorship of Richard Payne Knight (q.v.), the theorist of picturesque landscape gardening. Knight hired Cozens to accompany him on the tour and provide drawings of the various sites. The sketchbook Cozens completed for Knight contained some 57 drawings that are now scattered. *Between Chamonix and Martigny*, one of the earliest works from this tour, records the artist's confrontation with the Alps. Andrew Wilton believes that, although signed and dated on the back "August 30, 1776," the drawing was probably finished from pencil sketches made on-the-spot, such as the group on tracing paper now in the Yale Center for British Art.[1]

Despite the cool, monochromatic washes defining the mountain slopes, the lines of the composition are potent and energetic. The scene is devoid of anecdote, concentrating on the mountains themselves. Punctuated with staccato pine trees, the swift, downward sweep of the foothills emphasizes the dramatic incline of the mountain peak towards the jagged snow-capped pinnacle. The mountain range stretches into the distance and beyond the sides of the picture space, reinforcing the impression of vast scale and space.

Previous watercolorists articulated their paintings with strictly defined pencil outlines and opaque local color within the guidelines. Cozens' drawing, however, is very summary, with broad, transparent washes of grey ranging from cool grey-green to hints of ochre. For details of trees and rock he dapples the wet surfaces with touches of denser pigment to achieve the desired effect.

A small group of Cozens' contemporaries recognized the importance of his innovations in sublime mountain imagery and wash techniques. Near the end of his life Cozens suffered a debilitating mental illness that left him in the care of Dr. Thomas Monro, who was one such interested connoisseur. Dr. Monro collected Cozens' works and for several years held an informal ''academy'' at his home where many younger watercolorists got a start copying from Cozens' originals. One of these younger artists was Joseph M.W. Turner, who copied this drawing at the academy in 1795[2] and thereby became intimate with Cozens' iconography and techniques for mountain scenery.

1. Wilton, 1980a.
2. Ibid., 39.

37. Joseph Wright of Derby (British, 1734-97). *Derwentwater, with Skiddaw in the Distance* (1795-96), oil on canvas, 22 " × 31½ ". Yale Center for British Art, New Haven, Connecticut, Paul Mellon Collection.

After starting his professional career as a portrait painter in the 1750s, Wright of Derby turned to genre paintings of science and industry in the 1760s. Usually grouping figures around a bright artificial light, Wright would surround his scientists and laborers with dark, shadowy interiors. Wright introduced Caravaggio's *tenebroso* to English art at the service of romantic genre painting. On his grand tour of Italy, Wright was confronted with the cataclysm of Vesuvius erupting in 1774. His renderings of the lava-torched mountainsides are unique notes in landscape painting of the day. Like Wilson before him, Wright met Claude-Joseph

Vernet in Italy, who helped confirm his conversion to landscape painting. Upon his return to England, Wright retired to his native Peak District to paint landscapes and portraits.[1]

Late in life Wright toured the Lake District. He evidently enjoyed his trip and returned the next summer in 1794. The result was a small series of views notable for their adherence to picturesque stereotypes. Of the group only *Derwentwater, with Skiddaw in the Distance* (1795-96) conveys a sense of drama in the rushing clouds and rugged mountains. In this scene Wright has discarded the picturesque foreground to project the viewer over the lake. The sharp wedge of the rocky hillside at right interrrupts the view to the cloud-covered peak of Skiddaw. The sweep of the approaching storm parallels the incline of the prominent mountains and reinforces the scene's dynamism. Although Benedict Nicolson characterizes the late Lake District paintings as conventional picturesque views,[2] the dramatic activity in this depiction of Derwentwater seems a more sublime interpretation of the Lake District.[3]

1. Benedict Nicolson.
2. Ibid., 93.
3. Hawes, 11 & 116.

38. Joseph M.W. Turner. *Chamonix* (ca. 1809), watercolor, 11 " × 15½ ". The Taft Museum, Cincinnati, Ohio, Gift of Mr. and Mrs. Charles Phelps Taft.

The quickly approaching storm whips the wind around the mountainside, sending some tortured pine trees crashing down. Shepherds in the foreground scurry to round up their flock and lead them to safety. Along the mountainside streaks of sunlight pierce the clouds, highlighting the snowbanks on the vertiginous incline that looks up to the Mer de Glace. Turner enthusiastically recorded this and many other Swiss scenes while on his grand tour in 1802. In the four sketchbooks he filled with drawings, the great majority are views in the Alps. When he returned to England, Turner created a series of Swiss mountain scenes that are among the most dramatically sublime interpretations of mountains in British painting. Turner's earliest mountain paintings were inspired by trips to Wales, the north counties, and the Lake District during the summers of 1795-97. Although earlier scenes such as *Dolbadern Castle* (Royal Academy, 1800) were dark and moody landscapes, they do not approach the terrific intensity of his Swiss paintings.

The watercolors Turner worked up from his Swiss sketchbooks were among the highlights at the Academy exhibitions, from the sublime *Glacier and Source of the Arveron* (1803, Yale Center for British Art)[1] to the historical painting *The Battle of Fort Rock, Val d' Aouste* (1815, British Museum)[2]. This view of *Chamonix* (ca. 1809) is a variation on the 1803 watercolor *Glacier and Source of the Arveron* and was probably the source for the 1816 print in the *Liber Studiorum*.[3] Heightened anecdote and greater definition of details distinguish this later watercolor from the earlier *Glacier*. The chromatic range contrasts cool blue skies with the warm earth and establishes a bright atmosphere. Turner achieves highlights largely by the deft use of subtractive techniques in which he was a master. He carefully used a medium to stop-out the snow banks, and he wiped out the streaks of light in the sky with either a brush or cloth. In the tortured limbs of the pine trees, Turner dug in his thumbnail to scratch away the pigment and paper, leaving an agitated highlight.

The tremendous impact of Turner's views of the Swiss Alps altered the status of watercolor painting in England and brought a heightened expressiveness to mountain imagery. No British painter achieved again the grandeur of Turner's Swiss mountain scenes; however, American artists, when approaching their native wilderness, were inspired by Turner's interpretation of awesome mountains. Andrew Wilton noted in his conclusion to *Turner and the Sublime* (British Museum, 1981) that "It was no accident that the school which took up Turner's ideas with the greatest enthusiasm and conviction was that of the American 'Hudson River' painters, who responded to the immensity and grandeur of the North American continent by producing pictures of great size and exploiting the most grandiose effects of storm, sunlight and vast space."[4]

1. Wilton, 1979, 341, no. 365.
2. Ibid., 345, no. 399.
3. Ibid., 344, no. 389; Wilton feels that the 1803 version is the source for the *Liber Studiorum* print; however, a visual comparison points out greater similarities with the later watercolor.
4. Wilton, 1980b, 104.

39. Charles Turner after Joseph M.W. Turner. "Little Devil's Bridge over the Russ above Altdorf, Switzerland" (1809) from the *Liber Studiorum*, etching and mezzotint, image: 7 " × 10⅛ ", 1st state. Indianapolis Museum of Art, Indianapolis, Indiana, Bequest of Kurt F. Pantzer, Sr.

40. Thomas Lupton after Joseph M.W. Turner. "Ben Arthur, Scotland" (1819) from the *Liber Studiorum*, etching and mezzotint, image: 7 ¼ " × 10 ½ ", 1st state. Indianapolis Museum of Art, Indianapolis, Indiana, Bequest of Kurt F. Pantzer, Sr.

41. Joseph M.W. Turner. *Rheinfels Looking to Katz and Goarhausen* (1817), watercolor and bodycolor on wash, 7 7/8 " × 12 3/8 ". Yale Center for British Art, New Haven, Connecticut, Paul Mellon Collection.

42. Sir Francis Chantrey (British, 1781-1841). *Landscape* (ca. 1819), pencil, 6 3/8 " × 9 1/8 ". Washington University Gallery of Art, St. Louis, Missouri, Gift of Mrs. Stewart Borchard, 1963.

43. Edmund Burke (British, 1729-97). "Inquiry Into the Origins of Our Ideas of the Sublime and Beautiful," in *Works* (Boston: 1826-27). Washington University, The John M. Olin Library, St. Louis, Missouri.

44. Robert Wallis after Joseph M.W. Turner. "Bernard Castle, Durham" (1827) from *Picturesque Views in England and Wales*, v. I (London: 1838). Washington University, Art and Architecture Library, St. Louis, Missouri.

45. W.R. Smith after Joseph M.W. Turner. "Chain Bridge over the River Tees" (1838) from *Picturesque Views in England and Wales*, v. II (London: 1838). Washington University, Art and Architecture Library, St. Louis, Missouri.

46. H. Adlard after William H. Bartlett (British, 1809-54). "Village of Dormeilleuse, High Alps" from *Views of Cities and Scenery in Italy, France and Switzerland*, v. III (London-Paris-New York: 1836). Washington University, Art and Architecture Library, St. Louis, Missouri.

47. Thomas Sully (American, 1783-1872). *Castle on a Cliff, In Imitation of Turner* (1814), watercolor over pencil, 10 3/4 " × 8 3/8 ". Yale Center for British Art, New Haven, Connecticut, Paul Mellon Collection.

48. Jacob C. Ward (American, 1809-91). *Natural Bridge, Virginia* (ca. 1835), oil on board, 23 1/2 " × 32 ". The Nelson-Atkins Museum of Art, Kansas City, Missouri, Nelson Fund.

49. J.T. Willmore after William H. Bartlett. "The Catterskill Falls (From Below the Ravine)" (1838) from Nathaniel P. Willis, *American Scenery*, v. II (London: George Virtue, 1840). The Missouri Historical Society, St. Louis, Missouri.

50. Thomas Cole. "Lecture on American Scenery," *Northern Light*, v. 1, May 1841. (Albany, New York: Printed by Charles von Benthuysen, 1842). The Missouri Historical Society, St. Louis, Missouri.

51. Thomas Cole. *In the Simmental, Switzerland* (1843), oil on canvas, 20″ × 30″. Spencer Museum of Art, University of Kansas, Lawrence, Kansas.

On his first trip to Europe in 1829-32, Cole made his way to Italy by way of Marseilles. When he returned to Europe a second time, he took the more traditional route through the Alps, and this painting records Cole's impressions of the power and majesty of the Swiss mountains. Possibly, Cole could have encountered an English painting of the Alps during his first visit to Britain, especially as he called on Turner at his studio in 1829.[1] Nevertheless, he recorded in his journal, "I have seen no picture that represented the Alps truly, and words are incapable of describing them. The imagination searches in vain for comparisons."[2] What most affected him about Alpine scenery was its combination of "savage grandeur and pastoral beauty,"[3] of sky-lined pinnacles and tiny villages of shepherds. In a letter of October 1841 he enumerated imagery encountered in traversing the pass of the Simmental that emerged in this painting, exhibited at the National Academy of Design in 1843:

Stupendous mountains with snow-clad summits, impending crags, black pinnacles of rock, foaming torrents, valleys of deepest verdure whose green slopes ascended the mountain sides to mingle on high with precipices and dark forests; shepherds and innumerable cattle, making the vales musical with the continual sound of their large sweet-toned bells, houses clustered in the depths of the valleys, or perched on the tops of precipices. . .[4]

In the Simmental mixes elements of the sublime and the beautiful to present a vision of man existing in harmony with wild nature. The vast, irregular mass of the highest mountain closely resembles in form the peak in Cozens' *Between Chamonix and Martigny* (no. 14). In contrast to the bleak, forbidding terrain of Cozens' unpeopled scene, Cole's landscape includes signs of man's peaceful relations with nature. The prominent tower in the foreground echoes the slender peak of the mountain, emphasizing the village's pastoral seclusion in the shadow of the vast Alps. The dynamic silhouette of the foremost mountain against a sky filled with giant rolling clouds is echoed in landscapes of Frederic Church (no. 38), who was Cole's pupil from 1844-48. In his late European landscapes, Cole explored nature's capacity to inspire religious feeling. As he reminded American tourist-painters in an 1844 article on his European travels, "The traveller is unworthy of his privilege, and forgetful of his duty if he extracts not from the scenes described some moral or religious truth."[5] The Alps held a clear lesson for Cole: "Wonderful and glorious are Thy works, Almighty God."[6]

   1. "Notes on Art," 12 December 1829; Noble, 81.
   2. Letter from Cole to Miss Maria Cooke, Lyons, October 1842; Noble, 229.
   3. Ibid., 320.
   4. Ibid., 229-30.
   5. Thomas Cole, "Sicilian Scenery and Antiquities," *The Knickerbocker*, v. 23 (March 1844), 241; cited in Baigell, 1981, 70.
   6. Journal entry, 17 October 1841; Noble, 228.

52. Russell Smith (American, 1812-96). *Pass of the Bracco* (ca. 1851-52), oil on paper, 8 1/4″ × 12″. Vose Galleries, Boston, Massachusetts.

53. William L. Sonntag (American, 1822-1900). *Mountain Landscape* (1854), oil on canvas, 32″ × 48″. Muskegon Museum of Art, Muskegon, Michigan.

William Sonntag was one of a number of gifted landscape painters to emerge from Cincinnati, the cultural center of the frontier Midwest. To discourage the young Sonntag from a career in landscape painting, his father sent him as a youth on a trip deep into the Wisconsin Territory. He returned determined to succeed in painting such subjects. During the 1840s he painted Ohio Valley, Kentucky, and Virginia scenery and also ventured into large-scale allegorical pictures in the manner of Cole's *Voyage of Life* series, which entered a Cincinnati collection in 1847. After returning from a second trip to Europe (1855-56), Sonntag settled in New York City, where for the next two decades he produced American and Italianate landscape compositions that consistently relied on panoramic scope and complicated detail.

A superlative example of Sonntag's dramatic mountain subjects, this painting is probably based on scenery in Kentucky or the Allegheny Mountains.[1] It reveals Sonntag's debt to the precedent of Cole in wilderness sublimity. Like *The Clove, Catskills* (1827,

New Britain Museum of American Art) and other Cole compositions that Sonntag could have known through engravings, the foreground is densely stocked with lichen-encrusted boulders and scarred, broken trees interspersed among hardy evergreens. Unrelieved by human incident, the awe-inspiring face of the American wilderness directly confronts the viewer. The dangerously unstable foreground, with its suggestion of a sliding mass of trees and rocks at the right, recalls mountainscapes of the British school, notably the work of Turner, which Sonntag could have encountered during his 1853 trip to Europe.[2] The 18th-century "terrific" sublime is also echoed in the implied gulf of space separating the inaccessible foreground from the huge mountain commanding the distance; a few great birds pierce this vast, fog-shrouded space. Sonntag's *Mountain Landscape*, like Church's Maine wilderness scenes, reflects the merging of realism and a religious understanding of divinity in nature that typified the mid-19th century American response to native landscape. J. Gray Sweeney has noted the cross-like character of the three spiky trees at left and the powerful presence of the mist-veiled mountain as "a prime emblem of a monotheistic deity."[3] Such symbolism satisfied the imperative of contemporary American culture expressed in Asher Durand's 1855 "Letters on Landscape Painting," to impress "the mind through the visible forms of material beauty, with a deep sense of the invisible and the immaterial," to follow those "lessons of high and holy meaning" imparted by "the external appearance of this our dwelling-place."[4]

    1. J. Gray Sweeney, *American Painting* (Muskegon Museum of Art, 1980), 62.
    2. Moure, 22.
    3. Sweeney, 44.
    4. McCoubrey, 111-12, 114.

54. John F. Kensett (American, 1816-72). *Upper Mississippi* (1855), oil on canvas, 18 1/2 " × 30 1/2 ". The Saint Louis Art Museum, St. Louis, Missouri, Purchase: Eliza McMillan Fund.

Kensett's two works in this exhibition illustrate the change in his style from an early interest in the picturesque to a mature manner now regarded as one of the purest expressions of the "luminist" trend in mid-19th-century American landscape painting. Like Asher Durand, he began his career as an engraver, but in 1840 he went to Europe to study painting. While in England in 1843-45 he painted numerous small studies of English scenery like the undated landscape in the Washington University collection (no. 60). Kensett later related to Henry Tuckerman that "my real life commenced there, in the study of the stately woods of Windsor and the famous beeches of Burnham, and the lovely landscape that surrounds them."[1] Painted with dark colors and energetic silhouettes, Kensett's English landscapes display a familiarity with the English picturesque tradition.[2] In these works he frequently offset dense, shadowed forests and shallow pools against wedges of cloudy sky. In addition, Kensett's use of rustic figures and farm animals demonstrates his awareness of British picturesque conventions. In his letters he wrote of "the true elements of picturesque beauty" he discovered in the countryside of England.[3]

By the 1850s Kensett had abandoned his early interest in dense forest interiors and developed a luminist style that, as Lisa Andrus remarked, "created a mood of perceptive meditation that induced the spectator to see the poetry inherent in nature."[4] This poetry involved the subject matter of the traditional sublime reinterpreted with a mood of repose, tonal harmony, and a softening, all-pervasive light. This 1855 painting of Lake Pepin south of Minneapolis compresses within a small canvas a tremendous vista. The traditional stage-like foreground is replaced by a silver sheet of water, drawing the viewer into a shimmering void stretching to the far horizon. The surface of the painting, in contrast to his earlier picturesque style, is now uniform and polished, eliminating the artist's touch from the canvas. Above all, the space of the luminist canvas has been flooded with a silvery, cool light that dissolves the rugged peaks and joins water and sky. The new emphasis in luminist art on space and light as natural emblems of divine presence transformed the older sublime into a contemplative experience of order, harmony, and repose.

    1. Tuckerman, 510.
    2. Howat, 1968.
    3. Ibid.
    4. Lisa Fellows Andrus, "Design and Measurement in Luminist Art," in Wilmerding, ed., *American Light*, 39.

55. Sanford R. Gifford (American, 1823-80). *Early October in the White Mountains* (1860), oil on canvas, 14 1/8 " × 24 ". Washington University Gallery of Art, St. Louis, Missouri, Gift of Charles Parsons, 1905.

56. Sanford R. Gifford. *Storm in the Catskills* (1863), oil on canvas, 12 " × 18 ". The Butler Institute of American Art, Youngstown, Ohio.

57. Thomas Hill (American, 1829-1908). *Yosemite* (1860s), oil on panel, 21″×14″. Fort Wayne Museum of Art, Ft. Wayne, Indiana.

58. Albert Bierstadt (American, 1830-1902). *Mountain Landscape*, oil on paper on canvas, 11″×15″. The J.B. Speed Art Museum, Louisville, Kentucky.

57. Thomas Hill (American, 1829-1908). *Yosemite* (1860s), oil on panel, 21″×14″, Fort Wayne Museum of Art, Ft. Wayne, Indiana.

58. Albert Bierstadt (American, 1830-1902). *Mountain Landscape*, oil on paper on canvas, 11″×15″. The J.B. Speed Art Museum, Louisville, Kentucky.

59. Frederic E. Church (American, 1826-1900). *Mount Desert Island, Maine* (1865), oil on canvas, 31 1/4″×48 1/2″. Washington University Gallery of Art, St. Louis, Missouri, Gift of Charles Parsons, 1905.

More than any other landscape painter of the 19th century, Frederic Church captured America's enthusiasm for the sublime wonders of its oceans, mountains, and forests. An avid traveller, Church visited not only such well-known sites as Niagara Falls, the White Mountains, and the Catskills, but also South America, Newfoundland, and Labrador. His restless career became the paradigm for the adventurous journeyings of Martin Heade, Albert Bierstadt, Thomas Hill, William Bradford (1823-92), Thomas Moran (1837-1926), and a host of other American traveller-painters. Henry Tuckerman remarked in 1867, "Enterprise is, indeed, a prominent characteristic of Church; he has had the bravery to seek and the patience to delineate subjects heretofore scarcely recognized by art..."[1] As Barbara Novak has pointed out, the difficulties and perils of such vigorous pursuit of magnificent landscape subjects added to the sublime attraction of the finished canvases.[2]

A student of Thomas Cole in the mid-1840s, Church derived from him a practice of close observation of nature, supplemented with extensive study of the natural sciences, and a religious belief in nature's power to reveal divine truths. Elected a full member of the National Academy of Design at age twenty-three, Church reflected in his success the advent of landscape as a pre-eminent genre of 19th-century American art. Church conceived of himself as an artistic prophet of America's Manifest Destiny. In the massive, panoramic canvases he produced in the 1850s and 60s sublime natural wonders are materialized signs of God's plans for the American people. Church maintained his mentor's belief that "American associations are not so much of the past as of the present and the future."[3] Church rendered the awesome spectacles of American nature as revelations of the country's brilliant promise and potential.

Church's powers are seen at work in *Mount Desert Island, Maine,* painted in 1865.[4] He first visited the mountainous island off the coast of Maine in 1850:

> From the highest peak...we could easily see Mount Desert Rock, twenty five miles off in the ocean; and the mountain on which we stood is seen sixty miles at sea...Far out in the offing, the soft, hazy blue floor of the ocean was studded with nearly a hundred white sails of fishing smacks.[5]

He used this viewpoint in the 1865 painting, but reduces man's presence to a solitary sailboat. The viewer takes his position at the foot of a veritable Rock of Ages, the foreground hub of a broadly oval design of rising forested slopes and wheeling clouds.

This composition bears strong similarities to the overall concave design of Turner's "Ben Arthur, Scotland" from the *Liber Studiorum* (no. 40). As in Church's painting, the rocky foreground in the print provides a base for the sweep of the mountainsides and swelling clouds that cascade over the dark horizon.[6] In this rare case, Turner does not include any human anecdote to relieve the impression of desolate wilderness. The drama of the scene devoid of man may explain why Church was drawn to this particular composition. The breadth of space, surging atmosphere, and dramatic forms in *Mount Desert Island* mark Turner's general influence on Church.

Like George Inness, Asher Durand, and Sanford Gifford, Church responded to the cataclysmic struggle of the Civil War with paintings that translated into landscape metaphors the longings of a country for union and harmony. Where Inness' *Close of Day* (no. 12) may be interpreted as a vision of tranquility that was only an optimistic dream in 1863, the sublime triumph of light over darkness in *Mount Desert Island* reflects the hopes of a nation for a new era of peace and plenty after a long and devastating conflict. William McKendree Bryant, writing in 1881, emphasized the unity achieved through light in this landscape:

> The peaceful quiet pervading the scene is the peace that follows the conquests achieved by the Forces of Light, and the splendors of these forces are only infinitely multiplied

and rendered the more intense through their reflection in the conquered domain. Thus we have in this picture the representation, not of exhaustion and dissolution, but of rich, vast achievement and multiplied vigor.[7]

1. Tuckerman, 370.
2. Novak, 1980, 27-28.
3. Cole, "Essay on American Scenery;" cited in McCoubrey, 108.
4. Huntington, 62.
5. Huntington cites Church as the anonymous author of a series of letters in the *Bulletin of the American Art Union* (November 1850) that record a sketching trip through New England, winding up at Mount Desert Island; see Huntington, 30-31.
6. Wilton, 1980b, 124-26, no. 32.
7. W.M.B., "Turner's Sunrise and Church's Sunset, at the Loan Exhibition," *The Spectator* (St. Louis), no. 37 (May 28, 1881), 527.

60. Sanford R. Gifford. *Rheinstein* (1872-74), oil on canvas, 31 1/4″ × 27 3/8″. Washington University Gallery of Art, St. Louis, Missouri, Gift of Charles Parsons, 1905.

Gifford was one of the most popular of the second generation Hudson River painters, as well as one of the most prolific—the 1881 *Memorial Catalogue* assembled by the Metropolitan Museum of Art lists over 700 of his works.[1] Raised in comfortable circumstances on the banks of the Hudson near the Catskills, he was influenced by the nearby example of Cole to become a landscape painter in the 1840s. Though his earliest landscapes are indebted to Cole for compositions and subjects, Gifford gradually developed an interest in the effects of colored light, wholly removed from the moralizing expression of landscape motivating Cole. For Gifford, "landscape painting is air-painting. . .The really important matter is not the natural object itself, but the veil or medium through which we see it."[2] This feeling for atmosphere, as well as the order and panoramic scope characterizing his landscapes, links Gifford's work to the transcendental luminism of Fitz Hugh Lane (1804-65), John F. Kensett (no. 54), and Martin J. Heade (no. 61).

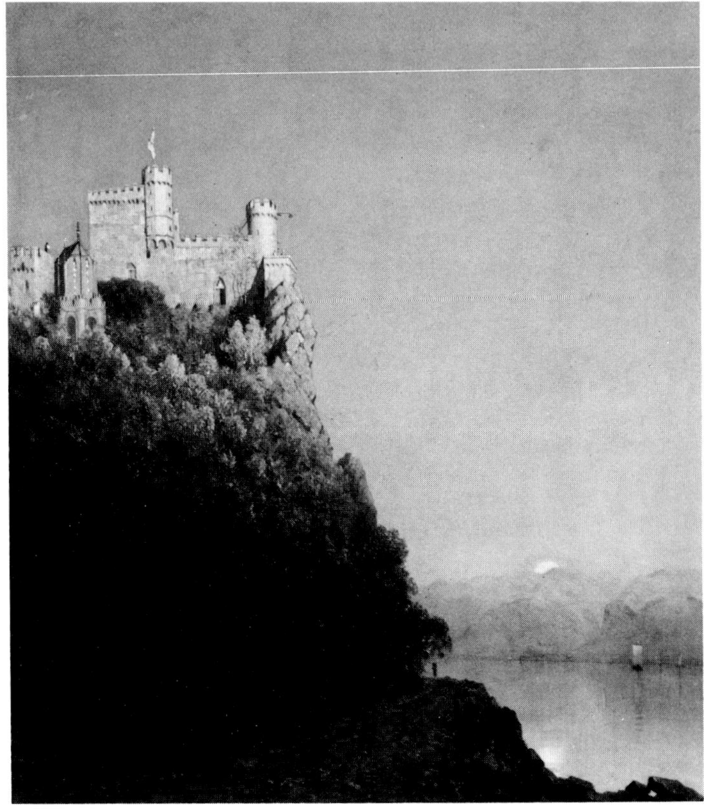

Sanford R. Gifford. *Rheinstein*, 1872-74 (no.60)

Gifford's concern with light and color appears in his transformation of a classic British motif, the ruined castle on a cliff, in *Rheinstein*. Medieval ruins figured prominently in English romantic literature and art both for their "picturesque" qualities and for the sublime associations they could inspire of "the transitory value of human possessions" (Sir Walter Scott) and "this world's

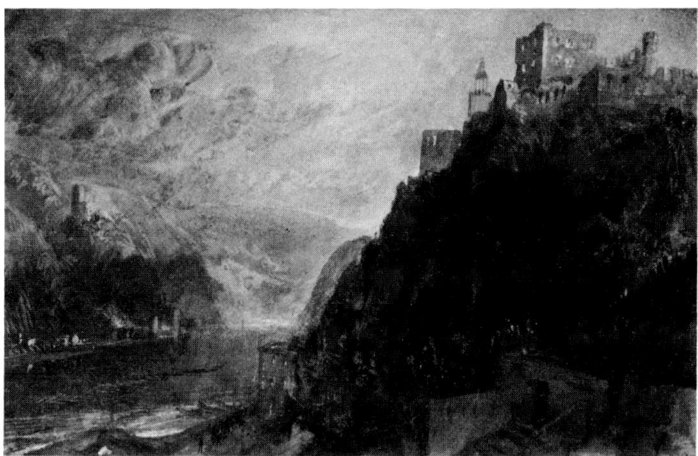

Joseph M.W. Turner. *Rheinfels Looking to Katz and Goarhausen*, 1817 (no.41)

passing pageant'' (William Lisle Bowles).[3] One of the most typical compositions using ruins silhouetted a lone tower or castle against a light-filled sky, as seen from a relatively low vantage point. Turner's diploma piece for the Royal Academy (1800) was a brooding vision of *Dolbadern Castle*, North Wales, on a darkened cliff beneath a threatening sky.[4] Turner's painting probably inspired the American portrait painter Thomas Sully's 1814 watercolor of a ruin astride a forbidding eminence, subtitled *In Imitation of Turner* (no. 47).

Gifford is notable among mid-century American painters for his keen interest in Turner. An especially dramatic use of ruins appears in Turner's watercolor *Rheinfels looking to Katz and Goarhausen* (no. 41), based on his 1817 tour of the Rhine. The craggy ruined fortress at the summit of the cliff overlooks a colorful spectacle of rolling mist and wheeling clouds above the hills on the far banks. During Gifford's 1855 visit to London, he sought out Turner's work and found watercolors of Rhineland scenery he recognized from engraved views. Gifford remarked in his let-

ters on their ''mostly brilliant'' color and light and ''extremely indefinite'' forms, and complained that ''the everyday look of nature is sacrificed to an exaggerated and brilliant blue and yellow look of color.''[5] However, as Nicolai Cikovsky, Jr., has pointed out, this introduction to Turner made Gifford aware that ''accuracy might be sacrificed for the sake of suggestiveness, poetry, and pictorial unity.''[6] When Gifford painted a Rhenish fortress atop a forested bluff, he showed it receiving the full illumination of the sun that has already partially dipped below the mountains. The castle is not shown as a hulking ruin, resonant with implications of the passage of time, but as a resplendent jewel celebrating a radiant present. The bright golden castle is contrasted to the darker brown tones of the densely foliated hillside and rockstrewn path below, as if to contrast sublime fantasy to picturesque reality, both joined in a poem of light. While the Turner *Rheinfels* is windwhipped and soaked in mist, the Gifford *Rheinstein* is serene and poised, a magnificent medieval vision held in the light of a cloudless blue sky. Gifford has yielded the associational power of a ruined castle for the presentation of a magic moment of the day, when the light of a setting sun transforms the architecture of man and nature into colorful spectacles.

1. *A Memorial Catalogue of the Paintings of Sanford Robinson Gifford, N.A.*, New York, 1881; cited in Cikovsky, 7.
2. George W. Sheldon, ''How One Landscape-Painter Paints,'' *Art Journal*, v. III (1877), 284, 288; ibid., 8.
3. Hawes, 35, 38.
4. Royal Academy of Arts, London; see Wilton, 1980b, 40-42.
5. Goldyne, 29.
6. Cikovsy, 15-16.

61. Martin J. Heade (American, 1819-1904). *Jersey Meadows* (ca. 1875-80), oil on canvas, 11 1/2 " × 24 ". Spencer Museum of Art, University of Kansas, Lawrence, Kansas, Bequest of Miss Edith M. Clarke.

62. Frederic E. Church. *Sierra Nevada de Santa Marta* (1883), oil on canvas, 40 " × 60 1/2 ". Washington University Gallery of Art, St. Louis, Missouri, Gift of Charles Parsons, 1905.

I. Primary Resources (chronologically arranged)

Thomson, James. *The Seasons.* (London: 1726-30).

"On Landscape Painting," *The New York Weekly Magazine; Or; Miscellaneous Repository,* v. II, no. 59 (August 17, 1796), p. 49.

"On a Taste for the Picturesque," *Monthly Magazine [American Review],* v. 31 (July 1800), pp. 11-13.

Knight, Richard Payne. *An Analytical Inquiry into the Principles of Taste.* 4th ed. (London: T. Payne, 1808).

Alison, Archibald. *Essays on the Nature and Principles of Taste.* (Boston: Cummings and Hilliard, 1812).

A.G.I. "Examination of Burke's Theory of the Sublime," *The Knickerbocker,* v. 2 (August 1833), pp. 113-119.

Dunlap, William. *A History of the Rise and Progress of the Arts of Design in the United States.* 2 vols. Original edition, 1834. (New York: Dover Publications, 1969).

"A Dissertation on Sublimity," *North American Quarterly Magazine,* v. 7, no. 33 (January 1836), pp. 80-85.

Ruskin, John. *Modern Painters.* 5 vols. (New York: Willey and Putnam, 1847-48.)

The Home Book of the Picturesque: or American Scenery, Art, and Literature. Original edition, 1852. (Gainesville, FA: Scholars' Facsimiles and Reprints, 1967).

The Crayon: A Journal Devoted to the Graphic Arts, and the Literature Related to Them. v. 1-8. (New York: 1855-61).

Tuckerman, Henry T. *Book of the Artists: American Artists Life.* (New York: G.P. Putnam & Sons, 1867).

II. Resources on Aesthetic Theories (chronologically arranged)

Hussey, Christopher. *The Picturesque: Studies in a Point of View.* (London: G.P. Putnam & Sons, 1927).

Hipple, Walter. *The Beautiful, The Sublime and the Picturesque in Eighteenth Century British Aesthetic Theory.* (Carbondale, IL: Southern Illinois University Press, 1957).

Nicholson, Marjorie Hope. *Mountain Gloom and Mountain Glory: the Development of the Aesthetics of the Infinite.* (Ithaca, NY: Cornell University Press, 1959).

Barbier, Carl Paul. *William Gilpin, His Drawings, Teaching, and Theory of the Picturesque.* (Oxford: Clarendon Press, 1963). Reviewed by Louis Hawes, *The Art Bulletin,* v. 47 (September, 1965), pp. 383-388.

Stein, Roger B. *John Ruskin and Aesthetic Thought in America, 1840-1900.* Cambridge, MA: Harvard University Press, 1967).

Sunderland, John. "Uvedale Price and the Picturesque," *Apollo,* v. 93 (March, 1971), pp. 197-203.

French, Anne. *Gaspard Dughet, called Gaspard Poussin 1615-1675: A French landscape painter in seventeenth century Rome and his influence on British art.* Exhibition. (London: Greater London Council, 1980).

Gerdts, William H. "The American 'Discourses': A Survey of Lectures and Writings on American Art, 1770-1858," *The American Art Journal,* v. 15, No. 3 (Summer, 1983), pp. 61-79.

III. General Resources on British Landscape Painting (chronologically arranged)

Manwaring, Elizabeth W. *Italian Landscape in Eighteenth-Century England, A Study Chiefly of the Influence of Claude Lorrain and Salvator Rosa on English Taste 1700-1800.* (New York: Oxford University Press, 1925).

Waterhouse, Ellis K. *Painting in Britain, 1530-1790.* (Baltimore: Penguin Books, 1953).

Hayes, John. "British Patrons and Landscape Painting — 18th Century Collecting," *Apollo,* v. 83 (March 1966), pp. 188-197.

Hardie, Martin. *Watercolor Painting in Britain.* 3 vols. (New York: Barnes and Noble, 1966-68).

Hayes, John. "British Patrons and Landscape Painting: IV. The Encouragement of British Art," *Apollo,* N.S., v. 86 (November 1967), pp. 358-365.

The Detroit Institute of Art and the Philadelphia Museum of Art. *Romantic Art in Britain: Paintings and Drawings, 1760-1860.* Exhibition. (Philadelphia: Philadelphia Museum of Art, 1968).

Herrmann, Luke. *British Landscape Painting of the Eighteenth Century.* (London: Faber and Faber, 1973).

Parris, Leslie. *Landscape in Britain, c. 1750-1850.* Exhibition. (London: Tate Gallery, 1973).

Burke, Joseph. *English Art, 1714-1800*. (Oxford: Clarendon Press, 1976).

White, Christopher. *English Landscape 1630-1850: Drawings, Prints and Books from the Paul Mellon Collection*. Exhibition. (New Haven, CT: Yale Center for British Art, 1977).

Bayard, Jane. *Works of Splendor and Imagination: The Exhibition Watercolor, 1770-1870*. Exhibition. (New Haven, CT: Yale Center for British Art, 1981).

Bicknell, Peter. *Beauty, Horror and Immensity: Picturesque Landscape in Britain, 1750-1850*. Exhibition. (Cambridge: Fitzwilliam Museum, 1981).

Hawes, Louis. *Presences of Nature: British Landscape 1780-1830*. Exhibition. (New Haven, CT: Yale Center for British Art, 1982).

Roethlisberger, Marcel. *Im Licht von Claude Lorrain: Landschaftsmalerei aus drei Jahrhunderten*. Exhibition, Haus der Kunst. (München: Bayerische Staatsgemäldesammlungen und Ausstellungsleitung Haus der Kunst, 1983).

IV. Resources on British Artists (arranged alphabetically by artist)

David Cox (1783-1859)

Roe, F. Gordon. *Cox the Master: The Life and Art of David Cox (1783-1859)*. (Leigh-on-Sea: F. Lewis, Publishers, 1946).

John Robert Cozens (1752-1797)

Wilton, Andrew. *The Art of Alexander and John Robert Cozens*. Exhibition. (New Haven, CT: Yale Center for British Art, 1980).

John Crome (1768-1821)

Clifford, Derek and Timothy. *John Crome*. (London: Faber and Faber, 1968).

Goldberg, Norman L. *John Crome the Elder*. 2 vols. (New York: New York University Press, 1978),

Thomas Gainsborough (1727-1788)

Waterhouse, Ellis K. *Gainsborough*. (London: Edward Hulton, Ltd., 1958).

Hayes, John. "Gainsborough's Early Landscapes," *Apollo*, v. 76 (November 1962), pp. 667-672.

Woodall, Mary, ed. *The Letters of Thomas Gainsborough*. (London: The Cupid Press, 1983).

Hayes, John. *Gainsborough*. (London: Phaidon Press, 1975).

Hayes, John. *The Landscape Paintings of Thomas Gainsborough: A Critical Text and Catalogue Raisonne'*. 2 vols. (Ithaca, NY: Cornell University Press, 1982).

Philip James de Loutherbourg (1740-1812)

Joppien, Rudiger. *Philippe Jacques de Loutherbourg, R.A., 1740-1812*. Exhibition. (London: Greater London Council, 1973).

Joseph M.W. Turner (1775-1851)

Finberg, A.J. *The History of Turner's Liber Studiorum with a New Catalogue Raisonne'*. (London: Ernest Benn, 1924).

Gage, John "Turner and the Picturesque," *Burlington Magazine*, v. 107 (January 1965), pp. 16-26.

Goldyne, Joseph. *J.M.W. Turner: Works on Paper from American Collections*. Exhibition. (Berkeley, CA: University Art Museum, 1975).

Herrmann, Luke. *Turner: Paintings, Watercolors, Prints & Drawings*. (Boston: New York Graphic Society, 1975).

Butlin, Martin and Joll, Evelyn. *The Paintings of J.M.W. Turner*. 2 vols. (London: The Tate Gallery, 1977).

Finberg, Gerald. "The Genesis of Turner's 'Landscape Sublime,'" *Zeitschrift für Kunstgeschichte*, v. 42 (1979), pp. 141-165.

Shanes, Eric. *Turner's Picturesque Views in England and Wales*. (New York: Harper and Row, 1979).

Wilton, Andrew. *J.M.W. Turner: His Art and Life*. (New York: Rizzoli International Publications, 1979).

Wilton, Andrew. *Turner and the Sublime*. Exhibition. (London: The British Museum, 1980).

Richard Wilson (1713-1782)

Constable, W.G. *Richard Wilson*. (London: Routledge & Kegan Paul, 1953).

Solkin, David H. *Richard Wilson: The Landscape of Reaction*. Exhibition. (London: The Tate Gallery, 1982).

Joseph Wright of Derby (1734-1797)

Nicolson, Benedict. *Joseph Wright of Derby, Painter of Light*. 2 vols. Studies in British Art. (London: Routledge & Kegan Paul, 1968).

V. General Resources on American Landscape Painting (chronologically arranged)

Sweet, Frederick A. *The Hudson River School and the Early American Landscape Tradition.* Exhibition. (Chicago: Art Institute of Chicago, 1945).

Flexner, James Thomas. *That Wilder Image: The Painting of America's Native School from Thomas Cole to Winslow Homer.* (Boston: Little, Brown, 1962).

McCoubrey, John W., ed. *American Art, 1700-1960.* Sources and Documents in the History of Art Series. (Englewood Cliffs, NJ: Prentice-Hall, 1965).

Callow, James T. *Kindred Spirits, Knickerbocker Writers and American Artists, 1807-1855.* (Chapel Hill, NC: University of North Carolina Press, 1967)

Novak, Barbara. *American Painting of the Nineteenth Century.* (New York: Praeger Publishers, 1969).

Howat, John K. *The Hudson River and its Painters.* (New York: The Viking Press, 1972).

Eldredge, Charles C. *The Arcadian Landscape: Nineteenth-Century American Painters in Italy.* Exhibition. (Lawrence, KS: University of Kansas Museum of Art, 1972).

McShine, Kynaston, ed. *The Natural Paradise: Painting in America, 1800-1950).* Exhibition. (New York: Museum of Modern Art, 1976).

Sweeney, J. Gray. *Themes in American Painting.* Exhibition. (Grand Rapids, MI: The Grand Rapids Art Museum, 1977).

Novak, Barbara. *Nature and Culture: American Landscape and Painting, 1825-1875.* (New York: Oxford University Press, 1980).

Wilmerding, John, ed. *American Light: The Luminist Movement: 1850-1875: Paintings, Drawings, Photographs.* Exhibition. (New York: Harper & Row, 1980).

Goetzmann, William H. and Porter, Joseph C. *The West as Romantic Horizon.* Exhibition (Omaha, NE: Joslyn Art Museum, 1981).

Czestochowski, Joseph. *The American Landscape Tradition: A Study and Gallery of Paintings.* (New York: E.P. Dutton, 1982).

VI. Resources on American Artists (arranged alphabetically by artist)

Albert Bierstadt (1830-1902)

Hendricks, Gordon. *Albert Bierstadt: Painter of the American West.* (New York: Harry N. Abrams, 1974).

Baigell, Matthew. *Albert Bierstadt.* (New York: Watson-Guptill, 1981).

Frederic E. Church (1826-1900)

Huntington, David C. *The Landscapes of Frederic Edwin Church: Vision of an American Era.* (New York: George Braziller, 1966).

National Collection of Fine Arts, Washington, D.C. *Frederic Edwin Church.* Exhibition. (Washington, D.C.: National Collection of Fine Arts, 1966).

Stebbins, Theodore E., Jr. *Close Observation: Selected Oil Sketches by Frederic E. Church from the Collections of the Cooper-Hewitt Museum, the Smithsonian Institution's National Museum of Design.* Exhibition. (Washington, D.C.: Smithsonian Institution Press, 1978).

Carr, Gerald C. *Frederic Edwin Church: The Icebergs.* Exhibition. (Dallas: Dallas Museum of Fine Arts, 1980).

Thomas Cole (1801-1848)

Seaver, Esther I. *Thomas Cole — One Hundred Years Later.* Exhibition. (Hartford, CT: The Wadsworth Atheneum, 1948).

Miller, Ralph N. ''Thomas Cole and Alison's Essays on Taste,'' *New York History,* v. 37 (1956), pp. 281-299.

Sanford, Charles L. ''The Concept of the Sublime in the Works of Thomas Cole and William Cullen Bryant,'' *American Literature,* v. 28 (1956-57), pp. 434-448.

Novak, Barbara. *Cole and Durand: Criticism and Patronage, A Study of American Taste in Landscape, 1825-1865.* Ph.D. dissertation, Radcliffe College, 1957.

Noble, Louis L. *The Life and Works of Thomas Cole.* Original edition, 1856. (Cambridge, MA: Harvard University Press, 1964).

Baltimore Museum of Art. *Annual II: Studies on Thomas Cole, an American Romanticist.* (Baltimore: Baltimore Museum of Art, 1967).

Merritt, Howard S. *Thomas Cole.* Exhibition. (Rochester, NY: Memorial Art Gallery, University of Rochester, 1969).

Wallach, Alan. ''Thomas Cole: British Esthetics and American Scenery,'' *Artforum,* v. 8 (October 1969), pp. 46-49.

Powell, Earl A., III. ''Thomas Cole and the American Landscape Tradition,'' *Arts magazine,* v. 52 (February 1978), pp. 114-123; (March 1978), pp. 110-112; (April 1978), pp. 113-117.

Baigell, Matthew. *Thomas Cole.* (New York: Watson-Guptill, 1981).

Jasper F. Cropsey (1823-1900)

Bermingham, Peter. *Jasper F. Cropsey, 1823-1900: A Retrospective View of America's Painter of Autumn.* Exhibition. (College Park, MD: University of Maryland Art Gallery, 1968).

Talbot, William S. *Jasper F. Cropsey, 1823-1900.* Exhibition. (Washington, D.C.: National Collection of Fine Arts, 1970).

Thomas Doughty (1793-1856)

Goodyear, Frank H., Jr. *Thomas Doughty, 1793-1856, An American Pioneer in Landscape Painting.* Exhibition. (Philadelphia: Pennsylvania Academy of Fine Arts, 1973).

Asher B. Durand (1796-1886)

Lawall, David B. *Asher Brown Durand: His Art and Art Theory in Relation to His Times.* Ph.D. dissertation, Princeton University, 1966.

Lawall, David B. *Asher B. Durand: A Documentary Catalogue of the Narrative and Landscape Paintings.* (New York: Garland Press, 1978).

Lawall, David B. *A.B. Durand, 1796-1886.* Exhibition. (Montclair, NJ: Montclair Art Museum, 1966).

Samuel Lancaster Gerry (1813-1891)

Hallenberg, Heather. ''The Lake of the Avernus and Its Elusive Mystery,'' *Muse: Annual of the Museum of Art and Archaeology, University of Missouri,* no. 12 (1978), pp. 49-59.

Sanford Robinson Gifford (1823-1880)

Weiss, Ila Joyce. *Sanford Robinson Gifford (1823-1880).* Ph.D. dissertation, Columbia University, 1968.

Cikovsky, Nicolai, Jr., intro. *Sanford Robinson Gifford (1823-1880).* Exhibition. (Austin, TX: University of Texas Art Museum, 1970).

Martin Johnson Heade (1819-1904)

Stebbins, Theodore E., Jr. *The Life and Works of Martin Johnson Heade.* (New Haven, CT: Yale University Press, 1975).

Thomas Hill (1829-1902)

Arkelian, Marjorie Dakin. *Thomas Hill: The Grand View.* Exhibition. (Oakland, CA: The Oakland Museum, 1980).

George Inness (1825-1894)

Ireland, Le Roy, ed. *The Works of George Inness: An Illustrated Catalogue Raisonne'.* (Austin & London: University of Texas Press, 1965).

Cikovsky, Nicolai, Jr. *George Inness.* (New York-Washington-London: Praeger Publishers, 1971).

Werner, Alfred. *Inness Landscapes.* (New York: Watson-Guptill, 1977).

John Frederick Kensett (1816-1872)

Howat, John K. *John Frederick Kensett, 1816-1872.* Exhibition. (New York: American Federation of Arts, 1968).

Joshua Shaw (1776-1860)

Woods, Miriam Carroll. *Joshua Shaw (1776-1860): A Study of the Artist and His Paintings.* Unpublished M.A. thesis, University of California at Los Angeles, 1971.

Russell Smith (1812-1896)

Russell Smith (1812-1896), Views of Europe 1851-52 and Later. (Boston: Vose Galleries, 1981).

William L. Sonntag (1882-1900)

Moure, Nancy Dustin Wall. *William Louis Sonntag, Artist of the Ideal, 1822-1900.* (Los Angeles: Goldfield Galleries, 1980).

Benjamin West (1738-1820)

Evans, Grose. *Benjamin West and the Taste of His Times.* (Carbondale, IL: Southern Illinois University Press, 1959).

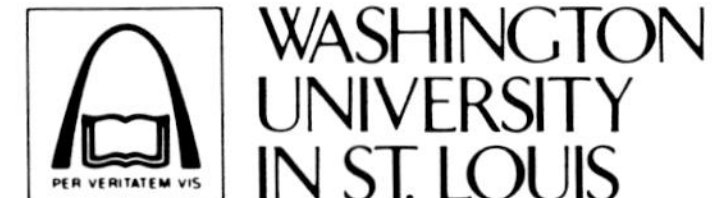